If your heart and soul have questions, about why we are here? What is our purpose? Am I going crazy? Are you open to a new way of thinking? If so, It is no accident that this book popped up.

> *Ann, share's her wondrous journey with love and wisdom. Her warmth and caring, draw the reader in, so that you can choose to BE and follow your own stepping stones. It will touch your heart and soul.*
>
> —**Deb Maslowski**

When I began asking my questions while on my spiritual path - "Why AM I HERE?" Many books and people came into my existence. Ann's book hits it all to the point of what we are all looking for "LOVE". The real message behind what Jesus was teaching. Its an incredible book of experiences Ann had with Jesus and of her many past lifetimes.

I am so glad Ann trusted herself and came to reveal these wonderful messages to us for humanity so needs it at this time. We are all waking up to who we really are... "LOVE".

> *A must read in my opinion and also tops on my spiritual book list for it comes from the heart and not the head. Bravo to you who pick up this book. You won't be disappointed. An inspirational and amazing story. I truly believe "Love" will be awakened in you once again.*
>
> —**C.O'Connor**

"This unique book reveals past life experiences of the author with Jesus (Jeshua). We feel that Jesus is talking straight to our hearts, helping us open ourselves up to the love of God and his love, which permeates our lives".

—**ML Franke, MD**
author of The Universe In Our Body

"Stepping Stones for the Heart literally exudes love and compassion for all who choose to read it. An inspirational and amazing story that is perfect for the time we live in now and for the future that lies ahead".

—*Craig Fuller,*
author of What if we were love and Pools of Truth

Stepping Stones For The Heart

Awakening with Jesus

ANN PAULSON

Stepping Stones for the Heart
Copyright © 2023 by Ann Paulson

All rights reserved. No part of this publication may be reproduced, distributed, or transmitted in any form or by any means, including photocopying, recording, or other electronic or mechanical methods, without the prior written permission of the author, except in the case of brief quotations embodied in critical reviews and certain other non-commercial uses permitted by copyright law.

ISBN
978-1-961250-38-3 (Paperback)
978-1-961250-39-0 (eBook)
978-1-961250-37-6 (Hardcover)

Dedication

This came alive for me somewhere in the tender side of my heart, in that place where precious memories are held in golden chambers

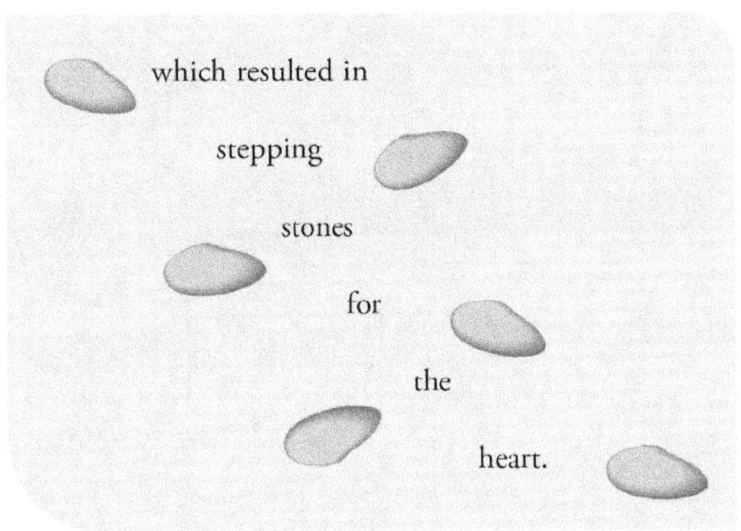

which resulted in stepping stones for the heart.

Table of Contents

Acknowledgements 1
Introduction 3
Preface 7

Part One 10
    The Beginning 11
    First Past Life 46
    Excursions I 60
    Second Past Life 79
    Episode II 93
    Third Past Life 98
    Interlude 119

Part Two 123

Bibliography 159

Acknowledgements

There was much encouragement needed to write this book. I thank my friends, Marlies, Deb, and Margi, for their continuous support and enthusiasm throughout the years in the process of writing. It kept me moving forward to finish it. Next would be my ever-patient husband, as I worked through revision and then another revision and rephrasing, etc. that a book requires.

Many thanks go to my daughter, Donna for using her graphic artist skills to create the cover. There are meanings to the cover. The flowers are Forget me nots, we are never forgotten. Purple is the color for spirituality and green is for fix its. We always have more to learn to fix old ideas.

And lastly, thank you to Jeshua, the angels, and other heaven lies. Jeshua definitely gave me information to write about.

Their continuing guidance, advice, encouragement, helped bring this to fruition. They definitely saw more to this than I did and probably still do.

Introduction

In October of 1999 my life, and how I viewed it and the world, took a definite turn. This was not something I was expecting, planning, or looking for. I began to experience definite meetings with Jesus, whom I now call Jeshua.[1] These were not physical meetings, but a combination of inner telepathy, trances, understandings, and visions. He gave me information to assist in my own present growth and also information about what happened in my previous lives that led me to where I am now in this life. In approximately four months I received the majority of this information. It took three years to completely accept it, digest it, or even begin to tell close friends about it. I suspect that you will need an open-mind as you hear my story. I have learned that not everything is as it seems, or as we are first told or taught.

    The book reflects the grand time that we are in right now. Whether we are aware of it or not, whether we want to admit it or not, we humans are on what I call an "alternating current" (AC) with the spiritual realm and within our earthly physical realm. We run the gamut as individuals. There are those of us who deny

---

[1] Jeshua is another name for Jesus. Jesus is the Greek form of that name while Jeshua is the Aramaic form that he spoke while on earth. This is the name I am more comfortable with in speaking of him.

anything spiritual, and some who are very committed to a spiritual path. The majority of us fall somewhere in between, thus the alternating current reference. The ego and mind place a veil in front of spiritual truths, which plays a part in our denial of things, thus the "negative" current. Spiritual awakening is definitely a "positive" current. Life is a balancing act between the spiritual and the physical; and now, at this time, we are all being asked to plug more and more into the positive spiritual current.

Spirit/God, angels, and Jeshua help us with the positive heavenly current. They are on the "heavenly side" and are always waiting to communicate with us, if we would shut down the ego or mind long enough, and ask for them from our hearts. We are alternating consciousness, trying to create balance in our lives between our physical experiences and the spiritual experiences. To experience and balance that current is part of the purpose of our lives. Maybe we won't get everything done correctly in this lifetime, but we are here to try, and to contribute our love the best we can.

From Jeshua

As I told you, Ann, my blessings are on the book, on all who read it and are open to it. It'll help them a lot maybe a glimmer, maybe a lot. They are the deciding factor always coming from the heart to choose. Choose. Does it feel good for you? Does it feel good for others? Does it feel good for all God's creation? I praise and thank God for his blessings to come through me unto this. You are loved.

Affirmation from Jeshua to publish this:

Get this book done and to an editor. Put the above in the beginning of your book. The above and the book are much needed. Your work on the book is not in vain. Remember, Ann, I said I'd bless each, and open hearts with it

Preface

My purpose in writing my story is to follow the angels' direction. Because of the times we are in, the added purpose in sharing this is to help those now "awakening" to gain insight into their own higher awareness and consciousness. In the beginning, when the angels told me to tell my story, I asked them, "What story?" They said, "A story of love". "As an insecure person in this area, I was unsure of this answer. I had no inkling of what was to come. I never considered myself an eager or proficient writer. This is definitely not about physical love. Rather, it is about love from and with the divine aspects that are all around us, and of which we are all a part. This is about the love which drives out fear and brings in light and truth. Perhaps in some way this story will be of help for others in raising their consciousness in order to experience the divine. Each of us is cared for very much and, in asking for the angels love, protection, and guidance, you will feel protected. It's only your thoughts, emotions, and feelings that can make it otherwise. I grumbled to the angels about this assignment of writing but they replied, "It will be a labor of love." And this is how it has turned out for me. I have heard from the spirit, and been told to write of the extraordinary things that happened to an ordinary person, me.

Spirit also describes this book as:

> *"God's spark is in everything. It works together, slowly mixing in, continuously unfolding."*

My central theme is a journey of a soul awakening and returning to a higher awareness, consciousness, and love. It is a journey I would never turn back on now that I have experienced it. Once you have been to this level of joyful revelation, it can become a piece of heaven on earth for you. Life on earth is a journey toward gaining this peace and a piece of heaven on earth for all of us. This is a joining of our physical realm to the spiritual, and ultimately to God. It is our evolution in spirituality. We are all on different pathways to this spiritual life and at varying points. Mine is a simple story. It was amazing to me at times, but I offer it to help you understand yours. We are in the new millennium where much angelic and spiritual energy help is increasing and offered for our paths.

As I tell you my story, think of yours. Think now for a moment, reflect on your life. Have there been instances where you felt that heavenly touch, that heavenly guidance? That's it, my friend, you have been touched by heaven whether you realized it or not. Now open yourself to it more and more. Perhaps in reading of my struggles, you will gain some insight, and your path will become a little brighter and easier. It can happen for all of us. With diligent work, prayer, sincerity of heart, and effort, you can be on a broader, brighter spiritual path, and higher spiritual consciousness that will also be reflected on your earthly path. Help is waiting, just ask your angels, Jeshua, God, or any and all in the heavenly realm with whom you feel most comfortable.

Author Joe Crane wrote that there are two ways of achieving the spiritual. One is by studying and learning, which eventually brings you to the spiritual. The other is receiving the spiritual first, and then you study and learn to understand it. The latter is what happened for me. If you say my story is hard to believe, that's okay. I would say the same thing, except I lived it and experienced the feelings and emotions of it. All I can do is describe, and if everyone could understand, feel, and experience the same things, the earth would be peaceful and filled with love. But, most important, what I do want you to do is to consider the things I learned in my beginning search and see how an understanding of these truths can be applied to your life. We live in such a great age. More and more people are waking up to the knowledge that they are children of God who deserve freedoms and rights and love, and they are bringing these concepts forward for the betterment of themselves and others.

I see myself as no more than a messenger to help you discover who and how great you are. In these times as you find these answers, your ever-growing, shining light will reflect back on everyone and everything, as we are all one. *Again - God's spark is in everything. It works together, slowly mixing in, continuously unfolding.*

Part One

The Beginning

Prior to 1999

Perhaps some brief background about me is in order first. I consider myself an average person, with an average life, an average IQ, and after looking at the same face in the mirror all these years, average looks. Even the gray hairs on my head look average now. My father was a dairy farmer and I loved growing up on the farm. I loved the animals, seasons, nature, and the freedom of roaming the land and woods. Much to my mother's consternation, I would just as soon be in the barn with the cows and calves rather than in the house. I had a rather tom-boy nature. My friends in town loved nature as much as I and would come for visits. We gave each other good memories of our adventures on my pony in the woods and fields. I kept my love of horses all my life. I always said somewhere in time I might have had a small transfusion of horse blood.

After college my town-bred husband knew I'd be happiest in the country and so our four children were raised in the country. An unwanted divorce found me raising four children as a single mother with all the related stresses and pressures. While my children did not grow up in material wealth, I believed in giving them a stable home life. This was to their benefit as they turned out well. I give credit to Jesus/ Jeshua for his help in raising them, as I asked him to help. When the kids were just about out of the house, I married a very kind and considerate man. About this time, heaven must have looked down and said, "Well, she isn't a taxicab driver for the children anymore; her personal life is settled. Now let's introduce her to something new."

I reiterate: I was not looking for, nor expecting, and knew nothing about the following which doesn't stop heaven when "They" have a purpose.

I held ordinary mainstream Christian traditional views and beliefs. As I went through life, I had my share of problems. I found that as we age, with more years and experience to reflect on, whether the problems where big or small, with heaven's help, we can survive them. Of the worst experiences, some that I thought difficult to live through, or others that scared the heck out of me, heaven was there, helping me in those times. I wasn't alone and neither are you.

Part of our reason for being on this earth is to experience the contrast of joys, happiness, work, satisfaction, sadness, worry, etc., that earth has to offer, and still bring out the higher evolving spiritual beings that we all are.

I have read and discovered that, before we came to earth, we planned the events, experiences, and people that we wanted to encounter on this particular journey. Considering the painful ones, I questioned, "I planned what? I wanted that?"

As I now look back at those difficult times, and how I emerged from them, I find myself stronger and more knowledgeable for having had them. We all have choices as to how we will react to our experiences. Our mind, heart, and ego give us choices on how to react. Which do we follow? I found that a new interior growth came my way because of the choices I made. Sometimes this growth can't be hurried but, with a new awareness of aid from the heavenly side, it can become less difficult. The heavenly side is able to see the whole picture, to guide us through.

One feature we were all given equally is free will. This extends to the heavenly realm as well as on earth. Free will is respected by the angels; they will not interfere with our free will. If we ask, they are more than eager to help in their loving ways, but otherwise they must stand aside and let us bungle our way through. The angels are now closer to earth than ever before to help us in our difficulties. Have you ever noticed the variety of angel material published or angel items that have become available in recent years? This is no coincidence, but it is their gentle nudging for us. So please, do be quiet and meditate, empty the chatter of your mind, and listen for their messages, feelings, a knowing, or thoughts that come to you.

When I look back (prior to 1999), there were times when I knew they helped me, however I was unaware or didn't believe that they were actually talking to me or that I could hear or sometimes sense their presence. I mainly dismissed it. This sort of thing was for saints, or extremely religious people not me. Ego can interfere by making us feel unworthy of help in this manner. No one is denied the angels' help; anyone can gratefully accept it like a spoonful of sugar to help the medicine go down, and defeat our egos and imperfect thoughts.

I like to keep things simple, honest, and most importantly no matter what find something to be grateful about. That just makes whatever day I've had go better. There have been studies done that demonstrate that by regularly doing this, it helps lift the mood. When things weigh us down on earth, we need to remember that what counts more with heaven, is our character, heart, love, intentions, and the choices we make.

We choose what kind of personal characteristics we will have before we come to earth in order to have the best set of circumstances to help us learn the lessons we came here to experience. Love is the main thing that we take with us from this earth and we need to ask ourselves all the time, "How well are we expressing love? How well do we love?" (I'm not talking lust here, either.) The minutest particle of earth, the universe, or heaven is made with and of love. I know my story could not have unfolded without love. After reading what happened to me, I hope you will believe in yourself as a spirit on an earthly journey, and believe that the spirits on the other side love and guide you. When you encounter amazing spiritual events in your life, be reaffirmed that these things can and do happen. Isn't it nice to think miracles can happen? Mankind is now becoming more and more aware of the spiritual energy dawning on us.

Previously dismissed strong encounters

Prior to 1999, I had few previous strong encounters with the heavenly side that stand out in my mind.

Once, as a young couple, my husband and I were strapped for cash that was dependent upon the sale of some property. I got an overwhelming sense of peace as I was praying that all would be okay and that this sale would happen. The sale did happen and it brought a big sense of relief.

On another occasion, I remember feeling that angels practically pushed me back upstairs in my house. They were trying to warn me not to make a phone call from the downstairs phone, regarding a big purchase that I really wanted to make. I didn't listen and I learned how important it was to be attentive to these sensations when angels were trying to influence me. Later, I found out that it was not the time to make this phone call. The unseen results of it were known by the angels but not by me.

There is a term called "cross channeling" that I discovered in 1999, though the unusual incidences I will describe happened in the mid-1980s and again in the mid- 1990s. In cross channeling, a spirit speaks through another person. It works in this manner: A person's vocal chords, lips, etc., are used by spirit to speak, but the person does not remember what is said. When this happened to me, I didn't realize at that time what was going on. I could see the people I was talking with, I could hear my voice, and I could feel my lips move. In my head were my thoughts, but my lips are saying otherwise. In both instances, the looks on the other people's faces were of astonishment, and I was thinking that whatever I was saying must be something really worthwhile. When I stopped speaking, I had no idea what I said, and I was terribly embarrassed. I hoped no one would question me about what I said, because to this day I still don't know. I was too embarrassed to ask.

In one instance, I was with friends and I knew their marriage was failing. After cross channeling happened, my friend told me I should write down what I said. In nervousness, I made light of the words I spoke (not knowing what it was). The second time I was at a staff meeting at work with five others. After the cross channeling happened, I just sat down in the farthest seat in the corner of the room, mortified, hoping no one would say anything about it. Again, I didn't know what I said, and wished I could dig a big hole to crawl into. One of the staff said later that I should speak up more. If he only knew!

I sure had no clue as to what else was working in those instances. It is so easy to dismiss the heavenly realm working in our lives, yet I've definitely found out that they sure are working within me. They are all around, for our own good to help us, and many of us are just beginning to fathom this. I admit though, it sure is easy to slip back into the structure of the world and lose this spiritual perspective. There are so many distractions, and spirituality is something that can come easily for some, and for others more effort is needed to obtain it. Maintaining spiritual perspective (a connection to the divine) is something that needs daily work to maintain at times. It's no different than if you want to maintain a good friendship or marriage. It is a daily thing.

The next big events started happening in October of 1999, and I was bewildered. One by one, my steps led to growing awareness and amazement. Because these experiences were so unusual, I didn't feel comfortable to discuss them with any other individual.

Much to my relief, by December I found a book entitled *Divine Guidance* by Doreen Virtue, which helped to explain all of this. My curiosity was peaked, as I really wanted to know more and more about what was going on. Over the years, I went from trying to understand, to integrating this into my thinking and feeling. Things changed as this interest turned into a spiritual mission for me. I wanted more knowledge of spirituality and how things worked in the world from a heavenly perspective, based on love.

I felt safer because it was based on love.

The Glider

"In the beginning amazement and wonder, in the end glorious."

~Jeshua

October 16, 1999. I'm an avid reader. My husband grumbles if my reading light is on at night when he is in bed trying to sleep. The subject matter I have been reading lately has been near-death experiences, angels, or other people touched by heaven.

I liked reading the *Guidepost* magazine articles because they are short and usually end on a happy note before I drifted off to sleep. With the approaching of the new millennium I had been reading the dire predictions in the tabloids. I discovered Ruth Montgomery had a new book out called *Worlds to Come* and chose to read that instead. Although I wasn't well acquainted with her material, I preferred her opinions as I felt she wouldn't be seeking sensationalism but the truth as she received it. Ms. Montgomery has many books to her credit which are of channeled material from her spiritual guides. I had read one of her books, and I took in what she wrote with a curious attitude. When I got to the chapter in her new book, *The Return of the Apostles*, things really started happening for me. I didn't understand it but it sure got my attention. Here is the passage I read.

> When Jeshua was condemned to death by the Sanhedrin, under Jewish law he could be stoned to death, and nothing more. The mob, led by the high priest, took Jeshua to the gates of the city, and they began to stone him. At the time, three of the Roman soldiers who were Herod's guards came by and the high priests pleaded with them to crucify Jeshua. This was the Roman way of execution. Because Jeshua was already half dead and could barely walk, he could not carry a cross too. These soldiers were quick to oblige, and of course the rest is history.

I thought to myself, *I didn't know about the stoning.* This had never occurred to me. I found tears just streaming out of my eyes. No sobbing, I had not worked myself into any emotional state beforehand. My mind questioned, *What's going on?*

The tears keep coming and coming. They didn't want to stop. I couldn't control them and I did not understand my response. My mind said, *It's just a paragraph in the book, but what a reaction!* Gradually I regained control and the tears ceased, but I still pondered, *What's going on?*

I had read Nick Bunick's book, *The Messengers*. He was businessman with no religious connections, and angelic things started happening for him. When I read his book, my reaction was, "If that happened to him, good for him," and I let it go at that. I found I had no qualms on what his book was about. I was not only intrigued by this, but it resonated with me. I felt this was the way it should be. Bunick also stated that more people are opening to spiritual experiences now than years ago, and those people alive 2,000 years ago are now back. Considering Saturday's events, I questioned, "Was I there 2,000 years ago?"

I felt an immediate inner knowing that I was there 2,000 years ago! This led me to amazement. To me, this is evidence that the veil separating heaven and earth is thinning.

While contemplating all the tears I'd shed while learning about how Jeshua was treated, and considering that people are coming back now who lived 2,000 years ago, my disbelief popped up and caused me to sarcastically think, *Oh sure, I was there 2,000 years ago. Yeah, I was at the crucifixion too.* At that thought, I experienced a powerful jolt of memory: I'm at the base of the cross, leaning on it for support. From behind I reach up and touch Jeshua's left leg. I'm surprised and shocked at how white and cold his leg feels. In present time, my mind was thinking, *What the heck is this?*

Much later, as I read more in my effort to figure out these experiences, I discovered a term retro-cognizant. It means your subconscious is helping your conscious mind to remember events that occurred in former lives. With a raised eyebrow I thought, *This is something new for me!*

Do you believe in reincarnation? It's true, it's a fact that doesn't require you to believe it either way. Buddhists have a saying about the "thread of life." This thread is the chain of life, of always being. We experience transformation, yes, but not death ever.

Before these extraordinary events started happening to me, I believed in heaven, although I never gave any thought to reincarnation. Americans are a minority in the world that does not believe in reincarnation. In the first 300 years of the Catholic Church, reincarnation was taught and believed. Then politics, councils, and an attitude that "my belief is better than yours" prevailed and the West was lost to that belief.

Now, more Westerners are learning about that truth. Reincarnation happens, not once but many times to a soul/spirit. I believe that God gives us as many chances as necessary to grow and develop holistically in spirituality. We all progress at different rates depending on our needs and attitudes. The earth offers a wonderful environment for this growth to occur rapidly, especially with the timeframe humanity is currently in.

I have connected the puzzle pieces together somewhat concerning what happens when heaven wants our attention, or at least, this is how it worked for me. First, there is some physical event that rivets your attention. Then you are swamped with love, affection, and a reaffirmation of their love and support. For me that love has occurred over and over, which kept me on the path to discover what was happening.

For me, a past life was revealed. Along with the amazement, the continuing love and support was expressed and given.

I must emphasize that words do not express all the positive feelings that occur as this progresses. Some people receiving this type of awareness back out of the world for a while. I did for about a year, and I delved into books on these topics to learn more. I tried to figure out what was happening. I'll share some of what I found in my readings that apply to my situation as I went through these experiences.

Eventually, if you are open to these ideas, you reach a certain point (after you have received the kind of help along the way like the help I experienced) when you are asked to continue your own development and path. But, the most important thing to remember is that you are still continually surrounded by support, guidance, and love from above. Sometimes I feel this support can be palpable as I continue to be reassured that this story is one that the angels want told.

The only time that this direct heavenly help stops is when you stop it yourself by giving ego the upper hand. All help is given in accordance with your free will, to be acknowledged in acceptance or refusal. I've wrestled with this so much over the years, going through confusion, denial, blocking. If I wrote down how many times, I told myself "This is crazy, this is nuts!" the remainder of this book would only have room for those two phrases. Twice I tried to just walk away from this and not having anything more to do with it. Both times I ended up tearing myself apart on the inside. You cannot deny who you really are which is love and still be happy. You see, love always wins out. Love, not just lust or emotional love, is the power in our universe God.

Two-and-a-half years after this "journey" started I found an article, "The Shaumbra Symptoms: twelve signs of your awakening divinity," by Geoffrey Hoppe. On reading this I thought, "More or less to varying degrees, I went through these twelve steps."

In case you feel any concern about the potential of experiencing any or all of the twelve signs, the heavenly side always emphasizes that you will come out of it okay. The steps are:

1. Body aches and pains, especially in the neck, shoulders, and back.
2. Feeling of deep inner sadness for no apparent reason.
3. Crying for no apparent reason.
4. Sudden change in job or career.
5. Withdrawal from family relationships.
6. Unusual sleep patterns.
7. Intense dreams
8. Physical disorientation—you are walking between two worlds.
9. Increased "self talk.
10. Feelings of loneliness, even when in the company of others
11. Loss of passion.
12. A deep longing to go Home, but first it is best to complete your life purpose.

These twelve signs continue off and on through every stage of ascension, or rising of consciousness. Hereafter, whatever I mention will touch on these twelve steps in some manner.

October 1999

Sunday. I went to hear a spiritual speaker. His basic messages were forgiveness and that more and more people are awakening spiritually than years' pass. Again, it was stated that those who were alive 2,000 years ago are now back. Driving back the many miles to home by myself, I start mentally debating about my being alive 2,000 years ago. Not finding any satisfaction in saying "no," I decide to try the "what if" option. Things really took off then for my spiritual awakening. This was the "crack in the veneer" that heaven was waiting for. Note, I'm driving my car down a four-lane highway at 65 mph, thus, there is no reason for me to be making this up at that time. Luckily, there wasn't much traffic. Without thinking about it, I start talking to the heavenly side. I'm discussing this with Mother Mary. I think of the private, all-girl Catholic boarding high school that I went to. Mary said that was the best "Essene-like" school at that time, and close enough to send me to. Now that takes me aback a bit. I never thought of my reason for going there entailed this, I was just following my parents wishes. (Mary was part of the Essene group. They were Jews but a different sect than the others. The Essenes were peaceful communities that lived in harmony with each other and the earth. One of their beliefs were they had been chosen to prepare for the coming messiah.)

Next, I started asking questions but I was really not expecting any answers. "What was my role, if I was alive 2,000 years ago? What was my name if I lived back then?" "Miriam," was the answer I got immediately.

After a few more questions, an overwhelming, sweeping sense of love for, or from, Jeshua came over me. It was incredible, it was deep. My amazed head said, "What's going on?" A voice (maybe an angel) says, "Welcome back."

I figured that must be in reference to my awakening. I just rested and enjoyed this incredible love I was being given. Again I say, "What's going on?"

The answer: "He (meaning Jeshua) is giving you a gift." There is so much incredible love, peace, joy, and happiness going through me. This is to be remembered. In my overwhelming feelings all I could murmur was a tiny "Thank you."

These feelings stayed with me the next four to six weeks, at varying levels of intensity. I'm not one who likes to display my emotions, but I felt like shouting "Jeshua loves me" from the housetops. Materialism or worldly things hold no comparison to this feeling. My reaction to this after the few days took two possible turns. Number one: a belief that all of this is true (how can I ignore it?), or number two I don't believe this or I believe half of this and consider it some kind of interior adventure. I chose number one.

I found I had no fear of death anymore. Why? There was this incredible love for him and from him. All the earth expressions of love fit in a small capsule compared to this experience. Then I wanted to express heaven's love, of which there aren't words to describe I could just feel it. He's up there and that's where I want to be someday, with him. I would have never said that before.

I feel such a bond of love there, and that love is returned hundred fold or more. I know there are others throughout the world and throughout history who have felt this way I now feel; if everyone could have just a few crumbs of this love, how the world would change to peace and joy.

An insight came to me what if my kids feel sorry for me during my funeral service? That would be so wrong because I would be as happy as a lark. I don't want anyone to feel sorry for me I would be back to our "real" home.

We may feel sorry for ourselves because we miss our departed loved one so much, but really, I would not want to deny happiness in heaven to those loved ones who have passed on. Those who have passed on have hopefully accomplished the mission they came down here to do, and now it is time to go back, back to their spiritual home, and the happiness it brings to them.

Remember when, on the way to the cross, Jeshua met a group of women and he said "Weep not for me, but for yourselves." That is it! He can't say, "I'm glad to leave earth" although he faces death; he's happy because he's going to be where he's the happiest (with his Father). That's why he could say, "Don't weep for me." He could see through the illusions of the world and continue on to accomplish his huge life mission.

This experience changed the way I feel about death. I haven't had a near-death experience like some have, but now I don't fear it. There is life after death and that life is blessed with love, joy, and happiness. The word for "death" should be changed to "transition," because that is what it truly is. It is a transition to joy and love. I never used to be heavily involved in "religion," and I don't experience this as religion per se. This is more like being involved in "spirituality."

Monday. At work, I had to keep reminding myself to concentrate on my job, for the euphoria continues. My mind kept wandering back to Saturday and Sunday's events. My face could be poker straight, but inside I was just happy, joyful, and full of love.

Now it seems like I could talk via my mind, with the heavenly side. And I could hear their answers. "This isn't 'voices'—these are thoughts, or mental telepathy."

Then it seems like I hear little congratulations being said all around me.

"Why?" I ask.

The return answer is, "Because of the place you had in Jeshua's life."

I wondered what that was.

At home, after supper I went up to my bedroom to be alone. I threw myself across the bed, put my head in my hands and pondered, *What is this?* I hear in my head *"You loved him"* (meaning Jeshua). I'm not really up to facing this I think.

Now I'm beginning to wonder if I am hearing all this, but the euphoria continues to remind me. Also I'm adjusting to inner locution. All this bothers me as I ponder, and so I can't sleep very well at night.

Tuesday. Today continues as yesterday, the same feelings and thoughts. Only now I start saying to myself, This is *ridiculous.*

I struggled with these concepts in the coming weeks. I tell myself if people only knew what was running through my head they'd call me crazy and nuts. I started becoming conscious of my speech so I didn't absentmindedly start talking to the heavenly side in front of others. I tell no one except my husband, and even then I don't say anything until Christmas. That was two-and-a half months before I dared tell anyone—to relieve some of this pressure! He knew something is up because I was up in the middle of the night, reading, listening to music, and acting like someone with a lot on her mind. He figured I'll tell him when I was ready. (He has been very supportive as I went through this. This is a huge A-plus from me to him because of his trusting attitude.) In the morning when I went to work, I'd feel there was a reason for all this; but as the work routine settled in by the end of the day, I'd say, "This is reality and that other is crazy."

The morning is a good time to feel positive about all this enlightenment. I discovered that it is in the wee hours of the morning at 3:00 or 4:00 a.m., that the mind and consciousness are clearest for the angels or spiritual side to work with me. We humans are attuned to the correct brain wavelength at that time, and so this can be the best time for the strongest spiritual communication.

I lost my assistant at work now for the next 4–6 weeks. It is more difficult to keep things going at work, and the staff probably feels that losing my assistant is the reason for my stress. That is the small part of it, but I have this interior mental fight going on that

I dare not tell others about. How do you go to your boss and say, "Excuse my stress; I'm just having an intense spiritual experience. I can't even believe it yet, but you can believe it," and still keep my job?

Besides, without my assistant, there was no way to take off. I'm not ill and there is no one who could really handle the job well enough on short notice.

Why do I continue with this? Because, through meditation I find joy, happiness, and love. It is like an elixir that draws me like a magnet. The bond between Jeshua and I grows immensely. His continuing love and support means more than anything now.

The third night into this, and for the next six weeks, I wasn't sleeping well so I got up in the middle of the night and thought maybe I could sleep better on the couch downstairs. Immediately, I fell asleep and I heard music. It was beautiful, harmonious, with a minimum of a four-part chorus of voices. They sang a very sweet, slow, and short song. There were just three phrases:

"I will fill your dreams"
"I will fill your dreams with wonder"
"I will fill your dreams."

Then I woke up and thought, If this is from Jeshua it's better than a dozen red roses and... I feel something important for me is taking place.

The music was absolutely beautiful. I asked others if they had ever heard music in their dreams and nobody I asked at that time had. But later in December, I learned that this was angelic music, and others reported having heard it. And for me the words turned out to be prophetic as my dreams or meditations were really making me "wonder." It was a neat wonderment though. I decided I'd sign up for the angel choir when I get up there, the music was wonderful.

Music is one of God's gifts of delight to the world.

~Jeshua

On my way home from work in one of those early days, I stopped at a grocery store. My frame of mind was in denial of who I was. All those little "Congrats" for my awakening were still flying around me. I slammed the car door and thought, *Great, I'm getting congrats for who I was* and I don't even know who I was. That stopped the congratulations. I felt the angels were a little disappointed when later I heard, *"Why can't you accept this?"*

The intensity of feeling decreased, but did not disappear. I understood that I would get further enlightenments but they would come more slowly so I could handle this better. But a new problem presented itself. I asked, "Is this new enlightenment real or something I thought up?" I thought it must be enlightenment because I didn't write or think that way normally.

While in my denial of the entire experience, I purchased a book to read as a distraction. I opened the book just to glance through, and these words leapt out at me. "Why are you afraid of my love, when my love has been protecting you all this time?"

Those words sounded like they were meant for me at that exact moment. The denial I felt was based on all kinds of fears. I wondered, *Do I feel I need the protection of love for what is going on?*

Immediately I knew, "Yes, I do."

Much later Jeshua gave me a saying, *Love drives out fear.*

The intense feeling of love I feel now is what I depend to overcome my fear of these awesome experiences.

There have been times I've just trusted Jeshua's guidance. I reasoned that he didn't do me wrong, so I decided to go along with his words on love. Later on, I felt Jeshua ask me three times in a row to trust him. Each time I answered yes. By the third time, I began to wonder what he was up to, and what would be asked of me. It reminded me of Peter in the Bible, when he denied knowing Christ three times. In hindsight, I'm very glad I became firmly seated in trust. Trust has been the most valuable asset throughout this discovery and I've called upon it many times.

Meditations

About three weeks into all of this, my mind was still reeling from all that was happening to me. Again I wondered, *What the heck is going on?* I was driving to work and still debating in my mind. *Where do I find answers?* I vowed, *I'm not going to admit this to anyone.*

You might ask why I didn't speak to a member of the clergy. But, at that point, the entire experience was really more than I wanted to admit to myself, and certainly not to another person. I'm just a mainstream person and not interested in theology or dogma. I thought these types of experiences and feelings happened only to gifted or saintly people, of which I am neither. Also I'm not at all interested in someone dictating "shall nots" and "should nots." Theology sounded boring to me and too difficult to understand. These new experiences were very real for me and I'm independent enough that I want to find answers on my own terms. So I turned to books as teachers, but there were so many and on so many differing aspects of spirituality. I asked for guidance on which ones are right for me to read at that time. As I worked my way through several books, more things started clicking for me. I found a lot of sayings about trusting your own instincts, intuition, or going with gut level feelings that those feelings are your higher spiritual self telling you the truth.

By the way, if you do this same exploration, make sure you are being absolutely honest with yourself and do not include the ego. Make the ego the servant to the heart. I found that my denial of these very experiences was really my ego working against my spiritual side. Now understand, my ego wants to survive on the things that it knows, not the new experiences such as those I was having.

Just to double check while I was reading, I asked the angels and heavenly realm, "Is this right, is this the truth? Is this how it works?"

The answer was a "knowing." I have continued to feel comfortable with the answers that come from the inside of me. The knowingness is real for me...I think.

I decided to try mediation using a CD I had purchased. I was not used to meditation or using music for that purpose, so at first this whole scenario seemed strange. Later on I got used to it and I found some songs that elicited very strong emotional outpourings from me. Never before had I reacted like that to music. At the start of these experiences I could and did interact with Jeshua. When I knew I had to stop the meditation to do other things, I became almost like a clinging child and did not want Jeshua's presence to go. I was afraid that his presence was a one-time occurrence and he might not come back, or I maybe wouldn't be able to feel him near me again. I am grateful that it hasn't turned out this way.

During that early time there was another part of me—remembering. My feelings and emotions were intense, deep, bursting, and with tears of love. Jeshua was understanding and patient, letting this pass for me. Sometimes we had very good conversations. I just blabbered away in amazement and ask questions. He knew this would happen and often put his finger to his lips to stop my chatter and just hold me. This wasn't a physical holding; it was more like a spiritual, ethereal embrace. Remember, he said, *"I am always with you."*

Now, all these years later, I don't have to wait for meditation to talk with him or with angels. If I concentrate and there are no distractions, it just happens. It is so nice to be able to do this. From what I read and understand, it will be natural and normal for many more people in the future to do so as well.

Other times when I am profoundly moved, a song will play on the radio with lyrics that are just what I was thinking or feeling it's uncanny. My reactions are AC alternating consciousness. I'm moved to amazement and joy at how all this is happening, and at other times, I'm in denial. In my denial, I switch the radio off and say this is crazy. You see I'm still interiorly fighting this. I accept, then I deny, then I lose sleep and yet have to live a "normal" life and face work the next day. I put myself through a struggle by not outright accepting this, but there it is.

At the end of my first session trying meditation I had two questions. Did I live 2,000 years ago, and if so, what role did I play?

I received a distinct impression that help was on the way. I don't like scary movies or books, so I told Jeshua if he gave me any scary stuff, I'd walk away from all this. He must have found my request to be amusing because he hasn't given me any scary stuff to date. I figured, *So far so good*.

I felt very uncomfortable with all this. I was not at all familiar with what was going on and I needed support with it. I also requested that for me to do more delving into the spiritual level he be at my side every step of the way as a guide. I might also mention that I'm not interested in relics or old moldy skeleton stuff. (There will be more on that thought later in the book.)

Have you ever been in a position where your back is turned and you can hear the people behind you talking about you? You don't turn around to acknowledge them because you want to hear what they have to say. About this time I had this sensation, but it was the spiritual realm talking behind me. Jeshua and others were discussing how now that I'm waking up, who is going to guide me. Jeshua stepped up and said he would, and so he has.

Another time in a similar situation, I heard a few observing that I sure came back different this time. I'm sure I did, but all I can be is myself. I don't know any different and would be a poor fake to try to be other than I am. Besides, they would know the difference up there.

As I sat in my glider the next time I tried meditation, I had a feeling that Jesus was sitting on the step stool of the glider. He was explaining reawakening to me. He said some things that were just beautiful. How I wish I had written them down, he is so good with words. He said "the veil is lifting" for me.

Afterward when I come out of the meditative state, I was taken aback that he could actually be sitting there talking to me.

I shook my head, trying to believe this although I had the distinct impression that it happened.

Several years later I asked him to repeat what he had said, the following is what I received.

> *You are awakening my dear one to forms and concepts you had no idea of. It is of how ideal you are to God. You may find you thinking of yourself as unworthy but that is your thinking. That is what you see from your place and time. We see much, much more. I love you as I love all on their journey and isn't a journey a time of growth and learning? This is what is opening now to you and to others. Although it may at times be confusing and troubling, in looking back you will see it as wondrous. Have faith my little one, have trust, call upon us (Jeshua, angels) to guide you. We do so with much love. Come my little one into the wonderful awakening of who you really are.*
>
> *All love, J*

I would like to reemphasize what he said to me could be said to you. We are all worthy, all loved, and awakening is offered to all of us with love and guidance. We are all so much more than we realize.

Methods in which this story was received

The majority of the spiritual knowledge that I have received, has been through meditations, dreams, conversations with the heavenly realm, automatic writing, and retrogressive hypnotherapy. I had not had this before, but I sure have now. Visions? Yes, but not with my physical eyes. It's with what is called an inner eye or third eye. Revelations? That's for sure. Below, I enlarge on some of these things.

The majority of what I receive is in meditation. I am amazed at how deeply a person can be in meditation. When I was young I had to practice it in high school and found it boring. I don't feel that way now, not after these happenings.

These days, I don't even try and meditation is so easy. I'd recommend it for everyone. It gives you a chance to slow down, look at and meet the inner you. Ask the angels help with this, they'd be more than glad to oblige you. There are quite a few CDs and books now to help you get started if you want to learn more about it.

When strong meditation occurs, you enter another realm or dimension. It's an altered state of consciousness and you are not very aware of your body or time. Everything just flows so naturally and freely. Things happen that I wouldn't normally do in everyday life. To say it is imagination—I don't think so. Writing is not my forte and being a fantasy writer is definitely not a category for me. The bond between Jeshua and I started close, and continues to be that way. He just has that way about him that, if you met him, you'd respond the same way. Many times he reassured me of his love and to not be afraid. He gave me lots of doses of love to help take away any fear. He definitely wanted me to remember these things so I could write about them. They are experiences to be remembered. At times I was astonished and overwhelmed by an experience with Jeshua, but love and joy were always included as well.

I had not heard of automatic writing, but I stumbled upon it in two books I read. The authors said that automatic writing is one way the heavenly realm communicate with us. I thought, *I'll give it a try,* as this is part of the adventure. How it works: you sit with a pad of paper and a pen, empty your mind of chatter, and listen for thoughts, feelings, visions, or knowingness to come to you to write down. This happened to me. I couldn't believe it! I had never heard of this before and boom, it happened. My original intention was to write down the experiences, but now I write down their conversations with me. I found all the messages to be very loving and supportive. These messages were definitely not my thoughts, because I don't write or think that way. After an hour or a day I'd go back to reread what I had wrote. All I could do was shake my head and say, "I wrote that?" The writings were good, and sometimes so loving that I'd have tears because the words stirred me so much. These are all consistent signs of automatic writing from the heavenly side. Samples of the automatic writing are those things in italics that were said by Jeshua or God or angels. Some are in the second part of this book entitled *Tidbits for us all.*

Now, a comment about dreams. In our physical bodies, we have emotions and thoughts that are also on the mental side on earth. We obviously know about and are aware of these. But we also have a spirit, a higher self, and/or soul that we don't see. They exist on the heavenly side, but both sides have God's spark of light and love in it. These ingredients make up the whole of us. Whether we acknowledge the spirit or soul does not make any difference, because it keeps communicating with the physical body, its invested interest. The soul knows all of our other lives and our present life's purpose. It will bring forth those things to the physical side via the use of dreams, familiar feelings, experiences, events, or places to help with our life purpose.

Some dreams can be confusing and we have to interpret what the signs or symbols mean. What I have written here is straightforward with no need to interpret what the statement means. We are, each in our own right, a valuable spiritual being in valuable physical form, and there's no reason why we can't have angels or the spiritual side come to us. They or God do not make any distinctions, only we do with our earthly outlooks.

Retrogression hypnotherapy is like being hypnotized, and the therapist asks questions of your subconscious about your past life. In the spring of 2000 I gave this some thought. I had never done anything like that, but in my head I heard Jesus say, "I won't let you" do retrogression. So okay, I'm not going to oppose the divine. Two-and-a-half years passed before I felt I was given permission to do it. I had to learn more, or be more accepting of this before I could do it. At that time, in the spring of 2000, this story wasn't really finished. In the spring of 2002 when I did do it, my reason was to explore further to see if the experiences I had where true. Would they be the same as what I got through the means described above? The answer was "Yes." The same events did come up and as a matter of fact they were enlarged upon. There was no way that my conscious mind could have answered the way I did in that session of retrogression.

The events of past lives didn't come to me all at once or in chronological sequence. I arranged the events of each past life together to maintain some continuity. In reality some of these things came a couple months apart and in random order. I felt Jeshua would inform me or give me a big revelation and while waiting for me to integrate that, we'd do other things. I call them excursions. This is how I have organized the book. There is a revelation, and then a couple of smaller items (excursions) while I'm absorbing the revelation.

A couple of times when my denial was too strong, the angels told me that they didn't want to lose me or for me to go back to my regular thinking. They kept with me, and I thank them and Jeshua very much for doing so. Again, if I wrote down how many times I told myself this is crazy, or this is nuts, or this is ridiculous, I could fill up the rest of this book with those negatives. I could have the most profound experience one day and be denying it the next. Thus in a dream, Jeshua told me about the AC the alternating consciousness, which I definitely did experience. These varying levels of disbelief carried on for two years. It was quite an interior adventure and I look back upon it with love. Thinking and feeling this new way is a normal thing to me now, a great way to view and live life. I find this saying to be true: "An adventure starts at the end of your comfort zone."

Another meditation

In heaven we can go places just by our thoughts. So in this meditation we change scenes with just a thought. In the second song while meditating with the CD, I found myself dancing in a circle with angels. Next thing I knew Jeshua was dancing along beside me in the circle, and we were in Jerusalem 2,000 years ago. I didn't quite know what the dance was but figured out later on that it was Middle Eastern. I can still see the quick, dancing sandaled feet, swirling robes, dusty ground, neutral-colored clothing, and the people dancing in a large circle, holding raised hands. It was outside and the tan walls of buildings are all around us. We were having a grand time, I could feel myself smiling it was fun.

Everyone was enjoying themselves Jeshua, too.

Right after this Jeshua and I were at my present small hometown church. The communion railing was actually taken down about forty years ago, but here it was up. In the sanctuary the tabernacle is on the left and he was standing about ten to fifteen feet to the right of the tabernacle facing me. I was in the front pew, facing him. He was showing me his sacred heart and there was a white light around him and it. He motioned for me to join him on the other side of the railing, which I did and stood beside him, facing out into the empty church. The white light spread to include me. Next thing I realized, he had his arms up and he was thanking his Father for my awakening. I respectfully stepped back to acknowledge his prayer.

Over time I debated why the communion railing was up and I realized that the railing was a symbol of separation. Joining him on the other side took away the separation from heaven and earth. Our present time is the uniting of these two, heaven and earth.

Then he asked me, "Do you want to go to Hades?" Hades is the fabled Greek underworld for the dead. I barely say that I've heard of the place and we were there. It was various shades of tan, even the air had some shades of tan to it. To the left were a couple of big pillars with marablized tan on them. To the right was a half wall and beyond that were human forms—they are also tan and looked like there was a giant nylon stocking pulled over them. I tried to make out any facial characteristics but I couldn't. There didn't appear to be any struggling like we hear about, and the angels told me that it's all soul work there. In hindsight I thought, *Let's do our soul work here on earth if we can, rather than wait to get to the other side to do it.*

I've learned that when we die, we'll experience what we think heaven is. If we expect it to be hell, we'll find that, gold paved streets, we'll find that, Christian their churches, Muslims their Mecca, Buddists their temples, and so forth. Here it is Hades and they get to think of what they did or didn't do before coming there.

There Jeshua was standing beside me and all of a sudden I thought, *What if they see us him and come ask for help? What do I do?*

Jeshua said, "They can't see us."

I looked at the people again to see more details, and all of a sudden I realized Jeshua wasn't there. I look around and thought, What am I going to do now?

I looked back to where Jeshua was and this long arm extended down and he pulled me up to him. Then we were in a sea. We were both sitting on something dark and slender. He was a little ahead of me on one of the slender surfaces to the right, and I was on another. We looked out, gazing at this sea. It was vast like a smooth sea, but it was not a sea. It was more like a grassy plain, but not really a plain, like a desert but not a desert. There were these little black stick- like things in it. They were two sticks close together at right angles, sticking up. I had no idea what they were.

Jeshua turned to me and said I helped him with this.

This visit with him in this meditation ended with that scene. Over time I kept wondering what those black stick- like things were. About three or four months later it came to me. Those little black sticks they were crosses, just the top two arms of the cross had been visible to me. All the crosses people have carried and asked Jeshua to help them with. He's helped them all and there is proof in the number it's beyond counting. Cool. What a neat way of showing this to me. As for my helping him, we help each other by our prayers.

In a later meditation

By the second song on the CD, again I was with the angels, dancing in a circle but on clouds. I was with them and then Jeshua joined in. Somehow he and I were now in the center of the circle. It was still a good time dancing; then the music stopped. He and I were still in the circle with the angels around us. Jeshua and I were still facing each other, holding hands. To me, this was going to a deeper level. It was absolutely quiet now.

Out of the corner of my eye, I noticed the angels were still there, but now they were sitting back on their heels, leaning forward with their wings almost covering their bowed heads. And I thought, *It is all because of him ––Jeshua.*

Again I noticed the quietness, the silence. Spiritual leader, Meher Baba, said, "Things that are real are given and received in silence."

Then Jeshua says to me, "All heaven knows of our love." I'm thunderstruck by that statement; but, yes, I'm feeling very loved. I'm puzzled by this statement, and then I explode, "All heaven!"

I'm shy and like to keep my feelings and emotions such as this to myself or the person I'm sharing it with, but all of heaven knows this? I don't think I like that. How am I supposed to take this statement? What does he mean? So I decide to look at it this way: heaven is built on love. Earth, like heaven, is also built on love. God's spark or light is in all of His creation, even us. If God calls himself love, then we are love too, being we carry his spark or light. Sometimes we just have trouble experiencing it on earth when we don't recognize it or let heaven in to help us feel it. We are caught in the illusions of ego and the grand, and the not so grand, of this world. Still Jeshua says he is love, and we are also love.

Against in the small hometown church

How do I know that the below things happened? I just know. The knowing is called Claircognizance in the metaphysical world. It's not with physical eyes; it's a knowing sense. From what I've understood from my readings, we humans have had this sensing all along. There are four ways of being in contact with the other realm. One is knowing (Clair cognizance). The second is feeling or sensing (clairsentience). The third is hearing (clairaudient), and the fourth is seeing (clairvoyance). We can have any one, two, three, or four of these. Usually there is one or two that are predominate at first until we develop the others better. It is how John Edward on his television program can communicate with the heavenly world. Small children, when they are born and for the first few years, are closer to heaven and have these abilities naturally. Instead of encouraging them in this, we usually close children down, telling them it is their imagination. We should instead acknowledge this terrific ability in children.

In the early winter of 1999 Jeshua asked me if I wanted him to go to church with me. I said, "Sure!" I sat on the right side of the church in a middle of the pew. He was standing between the tabernacle and altar, facing the altar, with hands clasped in front of him.

I thought what a surprise if the priest only knew what was going on as he was saying mass. When the priest said something about Father in Heaven, Jeshua raised his arms heavenward to praise the Father too. Rather than absorb and take glory for himself, he always directs it to our Father. After communion, there's room in the pew on my right and Jeshua comes to me and asks if he can pray with me. I say, "Sure," and feel complimented. He joins in the singing of a song. Without hearing, I know he has a good voice.

He kneels, forearms on the pew-back, hands clasped, head bowed, and prays, "Thank you, Father in Heaven, for bringing us together again."

I'm stunned by this prayer; my mind goes blank in reaction. He departs and I'm sitting there wondering. That's the second time he's thanking our Father in heaven for my awakening. It reminds me of his story about the shepherd going out to find the lost lamb in order for the herd to be complete. When a person reawakens spiritually, or when a person passes over, there is much celebration in heaven for each one.

With admiration I say, "Jeshua, you are something else." He replies, "Our Father is even more so."

Another thing I learned from this is that he really loves his Father in heaven. I never gave it much thought before; it was just words. However, after hearing and sensing this love, this truth is very strong. Any praise he gets, he directs to his father. Remember the story of the prodigal son and the father's rejoicing at his return? Perhaps this can be applied to us as the heavenliest rejoice with the spiritual awakening when we are able to see, communicate, feel, or know of these things. We, who are alive during this new millennium, are regaining these great abilities.

"You know, Ann, I came to earth because the Father asked me. He does not force, just asks. I also came because I wanted to. It (the world) needed help, and my love was focused on that and continues to focus on that. On its (the earth's) blessedness and continued blessed potential. All finds favor in God's eyes."

- Jeshua

Now remember that even though these amazing things were going on, I was still saying "This is ridiculous. What is this all about? This is hard to believe next to the realities of three-dimensional life." To be able to talk to Jeshua or the angels this way was amazing, and a thrill for me. My perspective had to, and did, change from rote, memorized prayers to actually conversing with the heavenly realm. It was a gift and, even though I'm more used to it now, I still find it thrilling. It is a great way to communicate, and I thank God for it. When you find this joy, then you are connected to your heart, which is the way our lives should be.

Spirit conversing

With this gift we can converse with others we have known and who have passed on in this earth life. I never really gave it much thought, but when someone close to me died, I felt like I could contact them to make sure they were okay. Since 1980 I have thought this way but did it only four or five times. I really didn't seriously believe that I was actually doing this. One day in the fall of 1999, I was driving to work, wrestling with all this, and I heard from Mother Theresa! She used the word "dear" a lot when she talked and I wondered if she did that when she was on earth, too. She said she came because I was having trouble believing that I was actually encountering Jeshua. She was trying to reassure me that I was. The essence of her words was, "He came to me in many different forms and ways in my earthly life," and that my encountering him in this manner was not only possible but true. Now I'm conversing with Mother Theresa! Expect the unusual as the usual.

Another reason that I was sure that Mother Theresa came was because she was a modern-day person. I mentioned before that I wasn't interested in old, dusty, moldy, relic, skeleton stuff. I have to retract those words (in the St. Rita section).

One night I felt Jeshua at my bedside. I just said, "This isn't right. He's only supposed to be so personal with really religious people," and mentally, I pushed him away. "He is supposed to be in some church, or talking only to exceptional holy figures or something."

So his presence started to leave. He used reverse psychology on me. I felt he was really leaving and that maybe I would not be able to talk to him again like this. As he was moving away, he said a couple of endearing words. I gave in. I could not push him away; I could not deny him, or the love he always brings. I've come to really believe and know that he isn't just a Sunday thing.

Even after the above, the next day I was fighting this again, deny it still working my way through alternating consciousness. If I hadn't been dealing with heaven, and had been dealing with humans, I would have been tuned out and turned off a long time ago. Later, changing my mind all the time became a standing joke between Jeshua and me. He does have patience and really needed it with me.

"The mind can change, the heart cannot."

~Jeshua

Spiritual foot in mouth

Sometimes in conversing with the spiritual, especially when I'm just getting acquainted with someone up there, I apologize ahead of time. I'm not sure how the other side works, so I just say I hope they understand if I stick my spiritual foot in my spiritual mouth. To me, that's a good basic understanding to have from the start. Long before all this started, I decided that if we're to go to heaven, it'd be a good idea to get acquainted with someone up there ahead of time—to make the arrival easier when the time comes. Jeshua got picked on by me and now he's returning the compliment, and I'm getting picked on.

One time I felt I'd stuck my spiritual foot in my mouth. Whatever it was, I don't remember now, the angels reminded me that I had been inappropriate. Of course, I felt bad and said, "See, I'm not good at this. I withdraw. I quit all of this."

Well, they didn't like that either and encouraged me otherwise. But I resisted. Then Jesus came and said to me, "What's this about?" I gave him my version and he just said for me to trust him.

I agreed that he'd never done me wrong. Just like that, I settled down. He has that effect. This episode and later on at another time, when I tried to deny this, I couldn't, and he said, "Love just won't let you, will it?" And that was true.

I've come to the conclusion it would be more painful to deny him and this love, and all the more joyful to accept it. Really to go against love would be to go against who we are, which is love, according to Jeshua. It would also go against God, who says that is what he is.

However, dealing with continual bliss and trying to act "normal" for many days became conflicting for me back then. So one day I got mad and chewed out God "Just leave me alone!"

God said, "Okay." I said, "I just want to go back to feeling normal. This continual bliss is affecting my work. I don't want to slip up among my work colleagues and say anything about this.

No one knows the whole story because I was still holding all this in. How could I talk about this when I couldn't believe it myself? I asked God that I not have those feelings during the day or, if I do, I could I please handle them better. And so, it happened. The connections of joy and happiness were still there, which I was glad about, but I was back to normal. Didn't Jeshua say, "Ask and it shall be given"?

One night, Jeshua came to me. In referring to angelic music and lyrics I heard, he said that I don't have to wonder anymore. I believed him, but my ego or mind didn't. I knew what the lyrics meant now.

I had been really wondering about this in the daytime and while I slept. My next challenge was to accept and believe all of it.

Another night he asked what colors I wanted my house to be. I was not expecting this, and I didn't know what he meant. I think he meant my heavenly home? Well, I went along with it and thought of my favorite colors, which were magenta or a dusty rose. Then he reminded me of a beautiful sunset I had admired on the drive home. It was a beautiful blue with whites, silver, yellows and gold. I said, "Yes, I liked that."

And he agreed. So, I guess that'll be the colors. I'd find out and write more about this later in other meditations about what the colors were leading up to.

By Christmastime that first year, I was in the positive side of AC mode. I wrote in my journal: "Such joy, love, and happiness at times. I know that it is Christmas, but when it isn't Christmas and I feel this way, I know I have a toehold in heaven. In an angel book, it is written that the purpose of coming to earth is to truly integrate the physical of earth with the spiritual of heaven. It's a task we set up for ourselves and have varying degrees of success in doing it. It's our choice and free will in doing so."

The whys

Different times over a period of the next six months I asked Jeshua, "Why me?"

I don't feel like I'm anyone special. Sometimes I think he's the shepherd, like the picture of him, and I'm just one of the lambs behind him going, "Baa, baa, baa."

One day he said, "You don't have to say baa anymore." Well me and my weird humor, I felt it humorous to continue the baa bit a little longer. So, another time when I was looking at the same picture of him with of a flock of sheep behind him, I heard him ask me which lamb I wanted to be. He's got his humor, too. I stopped my baaing then.

Another time I asked, "Why me?" I said, "There are others, and a person I'm thinking of about particularly, is more articulate, prettier, younger, energetic."

He said, "I didn't choose her; I chose you."

I persisted. "But she— is better at networking, social—relationships, and leadership."

He said, "You are pure of heart, like an open book." This was a humorous pun as I worked in a library. But what did he mean by "pure of heart"?

Later on I took it to mean that I don't have any other agenda than what I am about. Or maybe it's an innocence. In a sense I consider myself as a "what you see is what you get" kind of person. I would not consider intentionally putting down others to advance myself at their expense.

A few weeks later, the second time I asked him, "Why me? You are so smart. I'm not real good that way and know my flaws."

He said, "Even smart people need love." I had no reply to that.

Still later, the third time, I asked, "Why me? You are such a high level. You had to go through so much to get to where you are. There are so many different parts to you."

His reply: "You are right. There are many different facets to me. I kept a facet just for you."

I just accepted that loving response and replied, "I'm glad you kept that one facet bright and shiny."

I'm there for all, they just need to ask me and listen, observe, be aware of their feelings and intuition. I can come to them through that."

~Jeshua

Other experiences

In following the angel's desire that I share my story, I'll describe some of the more cherished things. It isn't all sober and serious when I talk with Jeshua. There's fun and word play. He can be as up to a good time as anyone. Of course, he can outwit anyone, but doesn't, and goes along with it in good humor. He relates to each person on his or her own level of humor, knowledge, culture, age, spirituality, and education. He can do this on a very personal level like a best friend. He won't do it unless you ask him, as he respects free will.

Edgar Cayce said prayer is talking and meditation is listening. I find myself doing that most the time now. It is not just intriguing, but something more happens for me with this practice.

A couple of incidents stand out in my memory. That's up to you whether you believe them; I'm just recording them. To me, they are amazing. Most of the time in these instances I'm aware of angels around me but they are very unobtrusive. I don't see them, but I'm aware of them. Also remember that when this happens, it seems very normal to me. When I come out of it, I think, *How could I do that?* or something similar. The following instance helped reinforce for me that these experiences were real. One night, while I was in my early resistance phase, I dreamed that those who had a part in Jeshua's life on earth were on earth now, and were together. The location was like a sanctuary in a church, and we were standing in a semicircle, facing an audience. The audience was dark and I couldn't see anyone, although I knew they were there. The walls were twelve-feet high or better, and were a golden, tan-colored wood. There was an altar toward the front with nothing on it but a cloth. Each of us stepped forward individually, with a light focused on each of us as we went forward. Each person said what part, or relationship, they played in Jeshua's life. These were all people who had a positive place in his life. I stepped forward and, with some courage on my part, stated what I was in Jeshua's life. While I did this, I half believed all of it.

An encouraging voice (angel? Jeshua?) said, "This is so you know," referring to the truth of what was happening.

Another time, back in Jerusalem 2,000 years ago, there was a feast outside in the same area that dancing was done. Jeshua was at the head of a long table and everyone was seated. I didn't know anyone but I took my place in the middle.

Across the table to the left a fellow says, "This is so you know this is true (what was coming to me)." I sure do need a lot of convincing.

First Past Life

Relationship from 2,000 years ago

I was going in circles, thinking of all that had come to me. Who was I? Why this? Finally, Jeshua tells me to put it to rest. These are his words on this.

> *Now write this down so we can say this is behind us. Yes, we were cousins on my father's (Joseph) side. You were somewhat younger, but in our childhood we played together as well as our age differences would allow. When I went away to study, you grew up more. When I came back, you had matured much. We then were able to form more of an adult friendship, and cousin closeness. We talked much as you wanted to know of my Egypt experience and you wanted to learn. You had an active mind– just wide open to learning.*
>
> *When I began preaching more, you believed me and helped where you could with my needs. We were able to discuss much more in depth and with awareness. My last three years were more intense and even when we couldn't get together to talk as much, you attended my talks and supported me. Before the last three years [of his life] is when*

we were able to share more, and more in depth when we could. Thus some of the experiences of us we shared. They are fond memories. You floated in and out with what they called the group know as holy women. You just happened to stumble upon the stoning. You knew my messages, believed them, and this [the stoning] was terribly wrong. Thus your strong reaction. You didn't know this was a divine plan, cuz.

Love, Jeshua

The above answer (of who I was) answered some but not all of my inquisitiveness about who I was. What did I do or what was I like? It was on my mind so much. Why did I have such a reaction to the stoning as mentioned in the paragraph while sitting in the glider? Those who were alive 2,000 years ago, and have come back at this time of millennium to be here for the changes that will come about, is the answer. (As a side note, I found that in reincarnation, people who shared their lives with others at other times come together to reincarnate again at the same time.)

I asked myself, Is this it with me? Why were there such strong reactions and emotions otherwise? What was it? I always felt close to Jeshua, but what was this? Was the stoning mentioned in Montgomery's book an incident from Miriam's life 2,000 years ago? The emotions of that sparked, and kept a very strong interest within me to further this adventure.

I'll start at the beginning of Miriam's life and follow through on what has come to me: Of all the instances in Miriam's life, I am aware that the stoning contains the strongest emotions of that lifetime. When Miriam was four or so, she was walking with her cousin Jeshua and some other children also around her age. Their garments were shorter, about mid-calf, because of growth spurts, which made room for skipping and playing feet. She remembers looking up at him and thinking even at this young age that she really liked this cousin of hers.

Later on when he was on a break from his studies at about the age of ten or twelve, Jeshua, Miriam, and a couple of friends were walking through a busy market place to purchase items. It's always a good time with him. It wasn't much different than kids and friendship and hanging around like we do today. It was just a fun day topped off with his sense of humor. We were making humorous comments amongst ourselves. He wasn't as well known then, but we said hi to a few locals. People shined up to Jeshua though, or maybe it was he who helped them to shine more.

At the revelation about the stoning he also told me that we studied the psalms together. It occurred to me when he said that Miriam was so willing to learn, maybe this is what he and Miriam studied together. In those days the only subject studied was religion. They were probably discussing items like this at another time in a boat ride on a lake. It was an unpainted weathered wood boat, like a rowboat. Because she was so eager to learn, he explained things to her, not just for the knowledge but also to see if she could understand the concepts. He had a faraway look in his eyes as he was talking of some concept, and she looked at him and said, "I like the way you talk." He looked at her, came back to that present reality, and then they continued to talk about everyday things.

At another time in their youth, they were sitting on a small boat dock ready to put their feet in the water and splash around. She said, "If you are a spirit, then put your feet in the water," because she wanted to see his toes. Spirits didn't have toes in her estimation. So they sat down and put their feet in the water. Looking down, there were her toes and, looking over to the side, there were his toes. He must have been amused at her sometimes. She must have been learning about what a spirit actually is for this incident to occur. On another occasion they were standing at water's edge, throwing rocks. He could make his rock skip a lot better than she could.

We are spirits in physical bodies. The bodies we can see, but the spirit we can't, although we know the spirit is there, helping and guiding us. It has also been called soul or our higher self. All that was coming to me, and my astonishment from it, fueled the curiosity in me to continue delving into books, to read, learn, meditate, and try to figure this out. My housework was really being neglected and I had to catch up. I got to thinking of how he said Mary had made the better choice of what to do by sitting by his knee and learning, than her sister Martha who was trying to manage guests, food, and whatever. I said their house must have been getting to be a mess too. Jesus replied, "Martha and Mary's house? Yes and no, as far as a mess, they didn't have as many 'things,' but food preparation and gathering of it was where a lot of the work went time consuming. There were not any of today's conveniences. I helped them with gardening and where help was needed. Rather odd to think of me milking or weeding, but it was done. Help was needed and I enjoyed it too. It was a diversion from my task of teaching and preaching. By the way, when we were younger, I helped you out a couple of times in those tasks also. It was how life was back then. There were times I sure was tempted to use my powers to get that weeding done faster though."

Another time remembered: I believe Miriam was twelve or thirteen and Jeshua was about seventeen at this occurrence. It was her job that day to watch the family sheep on the rough hillside.

There was more freedom in the Essene community for girls at that time compared to surrounding areas. The spring lambs were old enough that they didn't stay as close to their mother's sides. Jeshua came and sat beside her near the top of the hill to watch the sheep together and converse. One of the lambs went around the far side of a hill where she couldn't see it. During their visit she kept a lookout for the lamb, but it wasn't coming back into the open. Finally Miriam told Jeshua she had to go look for it as she was responsible for it. He told her to wait, the lamb would come back. After about the third time mentioning it, she said she better look for it, and she set out. It is downhill walk over rough terrain and about a block or so in distance. When she got within 100 feet of the lamb, it lifted its head from nibbling grass to look at her, and then calmly walked back to the herd. That darn lamb, she thought, *why did it wait till I was there and then decide to go back?* So Miriam scrambled back up the hill and over the terrain because Jeshua was waiting, and they could resume visiting. A short ways away from the top, she stopped (as she was out of breath) and looked at him. He was sitting there, grinning at her. *That fellow!* Then it came to her. He knew that when she got close to the lamb that it would turn and rejoin the herd.

Later on, when he was in his ministry of the last three years, Miriam came upon him in the Garden of Olives with a group of about thirty-five people around him. It had been a very long time, maybe a couple of years or more since the last time Miriam had seen him. He was in a cream-white robe with the hood over his head, and with a beard now. She noticed that he had an air of authority about him and he was on a mission to succeed. She looked at the faces of those listening to him. They seem captivated, and Miriam felt that this was what they needed to hear. The hood fell off his head as he stood to be heard better while he spoke. He was talking about goodness that there is goodness in each person, each person is blessed, and each person is loved… loved more than they know. Miriam looked at him with respect and again felt that she had one neat cousin. They had both been busy with their own lives, but after this she was more active in following his activities and speeches.

Miriam felt his mission was to explain things to people— that they didn't understand, and they had misconceptions.

Misconceptions that they didn't believe they were good enough, good enough to be worthy of the deep love God has for each of them. They needed to know it and look for it. They put themselves down. They needed love, love for themselves and for all others.

She felt that they understood at that moment what he was saying. It was so easy to in his presence to feel and understand that, but when they went back to their everyday lives and influences, this momentary understanding was lost and was difficult to put into practice. They did remember the words though, and how they felt at that time. That came back into play in their minds.

The karma of the stoning

One Sunday morning in January of 2000, I woke and sat up in bed. I had the strong apprehension something was going to happen, something spiritual was going to happen. *Something…*is going to happen. Then I lay back down and I was out like a light. I was back 2,000 years ago, and it came to me what happened in a Miriam's life 2,000 years ago. I was very much involved in this incident and although I tried to blame it on ego, my feelings and emotions told me it was true. Within myself, my higher conscious tells me it's true. The only other evidence of the stoning that I have found is Montgomery's book and the *Aquarian Gospel of Jesus the Christ*. Yet within me, this remains so strong. Who do you ask to find out about something 2,000 years ago that's not written anywhere but you know it's right? It's not in the Bible or Cayce's books. I asked three psychic persons who do angel readings. One wasn't a reading, but said I was there 2,000 years ago. Another said she could tell by my voice when I started describing it, that it was true. The third said that when there is emotion like that, it's true. Your feelings tell you what is true, and it must be that way for me because this is so strong and heartfelt to me.

This is what I received that morning: Back in Jerusalem on what we now call Good Friday, Miriam must have been walking out of town and saw a huge crowd by the gate. Wondering what was going on, she worked her way to the front to find it was a stoning.

Who was this happening to? she wondered. Then Miriam realized it was Jeshua being stoned. She was taken aback at these actions and shouted No! in her mind. Then she started shouting, "No," out loud and yelling at those throwing to stop. "No! Stop!" she yelled at them, saying that they don't know what they are doing. "This is wrong, stop!"

But it wasn't working. They didn't stop. She went running up to each of them, telling them to stop. It was no use. She tried to grab the rocks from their hands so they weren't thrown, so they'd drop them, but it was no use. She worked to the right of each person, trying to grab the stones from their hands, but they were stronger than her.

She wondered what she could do to stop this. There was much confusion and alarm in her mind. Her mind quickly switched back and forth from standing by him, protecting him, to her fear of getting hurt and watching what was happening. Her heart said, *Don't let this happen; do something, stop it!* But her mind said that stones hurt. Again her heart swung to protect him in some manner. "This isn't right, he is about love."

Finally with an act of courage and apprehension, but with commitment before she changed her mind again, she joined the melee. She went over and tried to cover Jeshua with her body. He's on his right side. Now there are two of them on their right sides. Miriam takes a few hits, especially one down by her feet or ankles. Then the stoning stops. Maybe they figure they're only to kill one person and not two.

Carefully lifting and swinging her feet, she moved over to the other side of Jeshua so she could face him. A thorn pricked her forehead as she leaned down to pick up his head and wipe his face. He had pain in his eyes but not fear. Miriam had terror in hers. She told him, "They've stopped," and she was so happy about that. He was safe and she was safe for the moment. She kept telling him, "It's okay, it's okay. They've stopped, they've stopped." The crowd was now standing around and was pretty silent, viewing the scene before them. She could still see the colors of the scene. There were muted colors of tan, gray, off white in the crowd's clothing. One side of the yard had a double line of people, one above the other. This maybe was a ramp. The ground was dusty, no plants because so many walked there because it was an entry to the city.

Miriam started speaking loudly to the crowd. "Don't you know what you are doing? I have listened to Jeshua's speeches. He taught love; do you call this love? He taught mercy, do you call this mercy?" She put in part of the Our Father prayer. "He talked of his Father to forgive our errors as we forgive errors against us. What are you doing? Aren't you listening?"

A man came forward with a stone to cast. She leaned her body over Jeshua's, waiting for fate to happen. But Jeshua in a firm commanding voice gave the order, "Do not harm this woman." He told the man to put the rock down, and the man complied.

Again the crowd is silent. Miriam looked at Jeshua in amazement; even in pain he had such a power, a presence. She tried to move so she could help him more, he was such a mess. Her feet weren't functioning well because of injuries, so her assistance was limited.

She cried out for someone to help them. No one moved. She tried to get help again, two times, three times. Again no one moved. Jeshua said he'd remember her efforts to help. She felt the dust and dirt, the anguish; and the emotional confusion came over her. There were a few familiar faces in the crowd, but they do not come to help. She knew he had inspired them, but they were held back by various fears of their own, of the ruling high priests who stood by and the Roman authority.

Then she heard the steady authoritative tromping of approaching feet and knew what was coming next. It was the dreaded Roman soldiers. Interiorly she cried, "No, darn it, this can't be. No!" While listening and waiting for their arrival, every tromp of their feet brought added dread to her heart of what would happen next.

They pulled Jeshua to his feet and led him away. He was in such tough shape. She wanted to help but there was not much else she could do. *Noooooo! It's not right!* went over and over in her mind. Tears streamed down her face and grief tore at her heart. There was such a gaping hole of sorrow as she saw them lead Jeshua away. It hurt so, so, much. That was the last time (I believe) that she saw him alive.

No one came forward to help. She knew there are people in the crowd who had heard his speeches, his teachings. He helped them and yet they allowed this to be done. There was such closed inflexibility in their thinking. They weren't free thinking and were so fearful, they allowed this to happen. Fear ruled them, and Miriam's sorrow continued to expand. No one came to help, even after she had put out so much at the expense of her own safety.

This scene ended in my mind and I was back in my bedroom at home with a feeling that Jeshua was at my bedside with someone else. He was looking down at me and saying, "We used to study the psalms together in the evening."

My eyes popped open. Was this a dream or a revelation for me? It sure felt very, very real. My emotions were raw. It felt like falling into a barrel of anguish and the bottom lid popped open and I fell deeper into another barrel of anguish. It remains the most emotionally draining experience I have had in my whole life. I felt numb after this experience and it took a while to recover from it. Dreams can be remnants of past life experiences and, judging from my experience, they definitely are.

Later on, the following came to me in continuing with Miriam's life. What happened after the stoning? Recall that while I was reading Montgomery's book (while sitting in the glider), tears had come to my eyes as I reached up at the foot of the cross and was startled by how white and cold Jeshua's leg felt. From retrogression, I found out after the stoning Miriam made it to the cross. But it was very difficult because of the crowd and her foot or ankle injuries. She found a walking stick and very, very slowly, but with determination, she walked to the foot of the hill. From the others that passed her going the opposite way, she learned that Jeshua had passed on. At the foot of the hill, she looked up and saw the three crosses, but oh, to climb that hill was going to be difficult. She was physically exhausted from the difficulty of walking. Then she noticed a lady friend walking quickly toward her from atop the hill. She offered to help Miriam get up the hill. Leaning on her for support, they reached the top. At the top, they were both tired from this exertion. There was open space around the foot of the cross and the friend led Miriam to the foot of the cross. She knew they were friends and the cross also afforded the opportunity for Miriam to lean on it for support. Besides, what is there to do now but say goodbye? Miriam touched his leg and looked up at his face. Such vitality, such love, life, energy, insight, wisdom, spirituality, humor, courage, love, and now…nothing… emptiness. She felt so so bad, as there will never be another one like him. She sadly surveyed the scene around her. Mother Mary was there with close friends and relatives by her. Poor Mary, Miriam sadly thought to herself. She had been to their warm family home a few times. Mary looked like she is holding up pretty well. Miriam wondered if Mary had a premonition about this. But premonition or not, nothing could really prepare someone for the actual event.

Miriam concluded that Jeshua's words needed to live on. *He should have written a book but didn't.* Why? Because he wanted to leave an indelible imprint on souls. That's why we need to go and find our soul, our heart, to find out what it's all about. Our soul is our internal guidance system, put there by God. We need to pay attention to it. He did.

Later on Miriam was sitting on the ground a ways behind the cross. Others came later to help her move. After that, and being a woman, she probably had to go into hiding because she had defied, reprimanded, and interfered with authority. Freedom for women in those days was limited, like it still is in some places now. She may have gone by way of water to hide, because I remembered hearing the creaking of the wood that a ship makes, sailing along. It ended up that the injuries or bones to her feet did not heal correctly. Efforts to help her were not successful. The word gangrene comes to mind. She looked up at the sky and there was an opening, a patch of blue sky. She thought, I'm going there, that's where heaven is. This is what Jeshua taught about. She passed on perhaps six to eight weeks after the crucifixion.

My emotions on this episode belong in the category of what is called karma. Sometimes just typing out this incident still bothers me. Each time as I worked through this, Jeshua came to help me deal with this difficult memory. The first time this all came to me, I just stepped back and looked at this and shook my head. Was I a fanatic follower to do something like this? No, I don't think so. I think, if you knew him, he just radiated love and you just couldn't help but love him back. He had such a presence. You would always remember it if you met him.

He gave me comforting thoughts about his death. I wrote down the following:

> *Even though I left you then, I am with you yet. Remember, feel, meditate. The water of life ebbs and flows, the love of your spiritual life always remains.*
>
> *~ Jeshua*

> *Spring is a cleansing for the earth. The timing of my passion and resurrection at that time also affords all souls a time for spiritual cleansing. Of course blanketed with love, as you desire.*
>
> *~Jeshua*

> *Remember my dear, we are about love. This love is you and me. This love is God. Love is who we are no matter*

what, where or when. Recall, remember—be at peace in your heart.

~Jeshua.

The following song verses are what I thought of when Jeshua was led away after the stoning.

Universal Salutation of Light and Peace Affirmation

> *I remember who I am.*
> *I am an ambassador of peace.*
> *My heart is the open door*
> *Through which divine love and light*
> *Pours into the world,*
> *Healing all wounds, Restoring peace.*
> *I remember who I am.*
> *I am love expressing itself*
> *Through all life everywhere.*

A lot of incidents in Jeshua's life were not written about. He could read and write but didn't leave a record of any kind. Why? Because he wanted the messages he spoke remembered, not the incidents that happened in his life. The message was the most important thing. He wanted to make an indelible imprint on the soul. Well, he has, on all souls of all time if they are open to him, or hear of him.

The following is a conversation I had with Jeshua about Good Friday.

Ann: Jeshua, can I ask? I don't want to be nosey, you can refuse.

Jeshua: Ask, Ann.

Ann: Okay, your reflections or feelings about Good Friday.

Jeshua: I ascended to my father, to my home in the heavenly plane. It was difficult—because even though those I loved on earth, I would meet in heaven—I was leaving them, and could feel their distress. But in the midst of the drama—the glory and joy I knew and felt—for humanity. Yes, I poured my life for them—but I left them with thoughts, a legacy—of my father's love, how life should work, of a chance—always a chance to live, to set their path on God's path. I did my best. Thanks to work, this was spread and others heard. Yes, it got twisted, but if you only knew, you do know on this side (heaven), the affects it had for humanity. You have a taste of it; there is more. Mission accomplished with great love. That love is still there today and all days, for all that want to drink and attune themselves to it.

I attended an angel workshop in February 2001 after the above came to me. A portion of the workshop was about focusing our minds on someone we are to forgive. The tables turned on me. Instead, someone came to me interiorly asking for forgiveness. It was one of the soldiers who took Jeshua away at the stoning at the gate.

I can still see him in my mind's eye, sitting on his horse, which had stopped by the gate, and he turned back to look at me. His message was, "I'm sorry, I have a family and loved ones now, and know how much pain there can be to lose someone you love." I was not expecting this and just sat there at this workshop trying to comprehend.

I noticed a fellow in the audience about two rows in front of me. When it was said that people 2,000 years ago are back, he was obviously upset. Was he just awakening, getting confirmation on his feelings or dreams? Was he the soldier? This is just an interesting speculation on my part.

> Jeshua: *I ascended to my father, to my home in the heavenly plane. It was difficult because even though those I loved on earth, I would meet in heaven I was leaving them,*

and could feel their distress. But in the midst of the drama the glory and joy I knew and felt for humanity. Yes, I poured my life for them but I left them with thoughts, a legacy of my father's love, how life should work, of a chance always a chance to live, to set their path on God's path. I did my best. Thanks to work, this was spread and others heard. Yes, it got twisted, but if you only knew, you do know on this side (heaven), the affects it had for humanity. You have a taste of it; there is more. Mission accomplished with great love. That love is still there today and all days, for all that want to drink and attune themselves to it.

Excursions I

DIMENSIONAL TIME TRAVEL

Healing of Jeshua's wounds and karma

Karma can be about of many different things. It doesn't have to be sorrow. It can be joy, happiness, and love. This is how the stoning karma was handled for me.

We were in the heavenly realm somewhere, Jeshua and I. There was a line at our feet, between us. We were facing each other. I was asked to firmly cross the line between us because that would mean a definite commitment on my part of who I had been in his life 2,000 years ago. Even with all of this, I was still having the alternating consciousness thoughts at the time.

I'd been struggling with this. It was yes, it was no, it was *how can this be?* Behind me I was aware of angels. I wanted to be on Jeshua's side of the line but not for the reason he was saying. So I moved to the left of Jeshua and crossed over the line there. That way I was side-stepping the issue.

Jeshua said, "No, that wasn't right." I needed to go back and make a deliberate crossover in front of him to make the commitment. This was very hard for me to do, for if I did that it would be a definite yes that I played that part [as Miriam] 2,000 years ago. This was a deep and serious agreement for me. I felt encouragement from the angels behind me, and of course there was Jeshua's encouragement. It was still up to me to decide. They respected free will and would not force me. Well, Jeshua had never done me wrong, so after careful consideration on my part, I stepped over and said yes.

Jeshua then scrunched up to a square at eye level and then disappeared. I thought, *What the heck, he wanted me to say yes, I say yes, and he then disappears!* I started thinking of crossing back. To my left, an angel stepped over and said, *Wait, he'll be back.* I waited and shortly, sure enough, he came back, and stood in front of me. He said that because of the commitment I made, I'd now have a healing ability. I didn't know what that meant except the following scene that has definitely stayed with me: Jeshua was sitting semi-reclined and I was standing to his left. He extended his left arm and hand out to me. I gasped at seeing his wounds from the crucifixion. As he put his hand out, he said, "It hurt like hell when they did this [exact words]." I just said, "I imagine." It looked so sore and painful. There was evidence of trauma, bleeding under the skin, and an outside hole that was now congealed with dark blood. With compassion, I ask myself, *What to do to help?* I almost touched his hand with my left hand to support it. With my right hand about an inch above his forearm, I brought my hand down. As I brought my hand down, the discoloration, trauma, and wounds disappeared. I was startled and surprised to see this happen. Then I thought maybe this healing would work on the other side.

There was dead silence during this and of course the angels were there, but out of my sight. I walked over to Jeshua's right side and he extended his right arm. There was the same trauma, same actions, and same results. I decided to try his feet. I knelt down by them and ask for him to extend his right foot. He did—same trauma, same discoloration, same actions, and same results. I asked for his left foot, he extended it. The procedure with the same actions was repeated, I almost held the limb and about an inch above the surface I moved my hand down the limb as it healed. I got up and went to the wound on his right side I moved my hand over it lightly, not touching it like I did before, and it disappeared.

The crown of thorns presented another problem. I decided that trying to remove it might hurt him worse. Instead, I decided to encircle my arms around it on his head, and the wounds healed, although the crown was left sitting on his head. It didn't bother him though.

I went to his back and asked him to lean forward so I could view that. I said this looked "mean" and he replied, "I know." There were welts, long strips of open flesh, congealed, along with redness, swelling, and discoloration. I took my hands and stretched them out with my thumbs together so I could cover the width of his back. Again my hands were about one inch above his skin and, as I slowly move them down his back, it healed. I was so delighted and glad that I could help with these injuries. Then I thought of internal injuries, but I didn't know what to do about that. My next thought was emotional support, so I went and sat by his right knee. I felt that if he wanted to talk about it, I was there and I would listen. Here this scene stopped, but the remembering of the words "love heals" came to the forefront for me.

Incredible, yes, but I would not make this up deliberately. I don't need to, it just came to me, I'm walking two worlds, and I won't forget it. Some of the results of this scene that came to me later were: Previously when I had reread that short paragraph about Jeshua's stoning, or if I thought about that event 2,000 years ago, I could still hurt emotionally. A few weeks after the above healing happened, I reread those words about the stoning or in thinking of it, and it didn't bother me as much. Then I realized that, because I couldn't prevent the stoning and all the wounds inflicted on him, the above scene gave me a chance to heal those wounds and myself. He was healing me. It healed my feelings and emotions on it, so I could deal better with it. Two thousand years later I was further healed from this experience. My motto changed from, "This is ridiculous" to "This is something else, expect the unusual as usual," and the love just carried on through this.

Jeshua is very real in my life now. I keep thinking that we need to get him off that crucifix and practice what he taught and lived. How many times have we had the guilt laid on us about how Christ died for our sins? As important as his passion was, it happened in less than a day, compared to all the other days he lived to teach us. One day he picked the subject of guilt to speak on. This is as follows:

> *"Guilt—There's a place for it: in the trash can. All need to know that God doesn't make junk, that [guilt] belongs in the trash can. We are all perfect humans or better spirits because God created and dwells in us. If we belong in the trash can, doesn't that mean God belongs there also? Sorry! He doesn't do that to himself and doesn't do that to you, his creation. Just the guilt belongs there. We commit error so we can learn and profit from this earthly journey and that is why forgiveness for yourselves and others is so important. You are all blessed. ~Jeshua*

> *Jeshua: My cross, my cross for you is now based on love.*

> *Correct?*

> *Ann: Very correct.*

> *Jeshua: Hold that in your mind, your heart, on your lips.*

Notice he didn't say based on guilt.

In thinking of this, all I can say is "What a lifetime, what events! Wow!"

About three years after this healing experience, I attended a class on healing. One of the hand positions was the same that I used on Jeshua's back. At that time I didn't know this hand position, and I marveled again how what happens to me in a vision or dream can come about in daily life. It's backup and proof to me how all of this can work for the good in the long run.

Excursions – Episode I

Who would ever guess I'd be in my own "back to the past" movie? As I mentioned before, Jeshua took me on excursions while letting information about the enormity of a past life could be absorbed by my mind. Below are a few of the episodes. I needed the shock absorber of time after these lifetimes before starting another one. These excursions were not related to a lifetime, just planned events by Jeshua. When I am with him, these events just happen and flow so easily. It's his energy, but maybe it's my higher spiritual self saying it's time for this, too.

Jordan River

In this one I was myself in the twentieth century with Jeshua, and we traveled back 2,000 years. This is another scene that moved me a lot and stayed with me for many feeling days afterward.

We were standing in the Jordan River of 2,000 years ago. He was standing beside me and he raised his hands cupped with water to pour water on my head. As he did this he said, *"As my Father blessed me, so I bless you with my blessings and love."*

My whole being stumbled at those words, and at what was being done and said. I was stunned, and could do no more than stand there with my head lowered. I was asked if I needed help moving out of the water. My legs felt like dead weight.. I made much effort to move and succeeded in getting to the water's edge to stand. I was too moved to think, act, or speak. Here was where he got "Christed," the first confirmation of his real life mission and he shared a similar situation with me. I asked myself, *Is this supposed to mean something more than I am aware of?*

Jeshua asked me to go up with him to the Father. I say, "Sure," but could hardly do anything. He offered to help but I made a serious effort and kept up with him.

What do I mean by "up"? My body was here, but in mediation or like in dreams, my mind or soul or spirit goes elsewhere and has these experiences. Everything just flows and when I come out I ask myself, "Why would I do that when in real life I wouldn't even consider it?"

In these meditations or dreams, the soul or spirit is able to relate to the heavenly world without the illusions of this earthly plane coming through. Although angels and Jeshua know we have faults here, they also know how we really are on the heavenly side, and that events we have planned for our earthly incarnation will bring forth the reactions and feelings from the lessons we learn here. From this plan they know we'll have good times and bad times, and so they relate to both. They try to help us raise our earthly side as far as possible in order to resonate with our heavenly side. This is no small task, I might add, as most people don't realize this, or like me, they deny it.

The intensity, feelings, and mood after the Jordan episode stayed with me for a few days. I couldn't shake this too easily. With just a thought, I asked his mother, Mary, "What was that about?"

She was a little amused and said it was a simple display of affection. My reaction to this was way beyond simple in that it impacted me so much.

The next time I was with Jeshua, I shyly but playfully baptized him with my love and blessings. He was sitting and just closed his eyes and turned his head to the side like this blessing was affecting him. I wondered, *What did I do?* I went back later and asked, "Are you all right?"

Of course he was but he said, *"No one has done that to me for a long time."*

I wondered if it brought back memories of when he was Christed.

Jeshua said, "It did, Ann."

Now I was no longer just sticking my spiritual foot in my spiritual mouth, but also my spiritual actions in who knows where.

Let's think outside of the box for a bit. Jeshua came into this world many times. Yes, he had more than one lifetime on earth. Remember, he said he was like us. Each time he worked to increase his spiritual abilities. When he came two thousand years ago he was just outstanding. He knew it, as those around him did. His connection with the Father was so absolute that he really became Christed to bring further enlightenment to man. When the dove and voice appeared as John baptized him, that confirmed what was going on.

Jeshua's real name is Jeshua bin Joseph. The bin is for son of. Christ means oneness—oneness with the father and mankind, as we are all one with him. After the baptism, Jeshua went for forty days out in the desert to think about things. On his return he was definitely one with the father and saw the rest of humanity in that oneness. What a journey the rest of us are on to get to that point.

Blessed Virgin Mary

When Jeshua introduced himself to me, I felt a familiarity with him right away. He is quite a gentleman. I believe he can be quite personal from the very beginning with anyone. I was thinking about how when you get to know someone, eventually you are introduced to their folks. I thought it was odd that I wasn't getting introduced to Jeshua folks.

He asked me if I wanted to meet his mother, Mary. "Of course," I answered. And we were then back in

Jerusalem 2,000 years ago, but in my present mind. We were outside his mother's house, standing on a slight slope by the side of the house as she rounded the corner to meet us outside. I was stunned and had no idea what to say. She quickly summed up the situation and told Jeshua, "You need to spend more time reacquainting with each other in the twentieth-century timeframe," and so we did.

With just a thought, we were somewhere by ourselves. I don't know where, but it was in the country with huge, old, deciduous trees on each side of the road. It was just a small, dirt country road between the two rows of trees. There was a small space between the road and trees with grassy fields beyond that. We leaned against a tree and visited. It was so peaceful, with nice weather and the best of company to be with.

Winter of 2000

One Sunday morning I asked Jeshua what he did on Sunday mornings since I knew church services are conducted then. This is what follows:

The scene was bright with some greenery to the distant left extending to center front, with a light-gray sky. The floor was bubbles. The bubbles were oval like a capsule but very clear and they were all the same size. They were arranged in rows, end to end, and more than one layer thick. More bubbles kept arriving and arranging themselves in order. In these bubbles were peoples' thoughts, requests, or petitions as they said them in their churches or minds.

The requests weren't written on paper, they were just black letters of the alphabet arranged to spell the words, sentences, prayers, and thoughts. Some had little scenes, like videos in them. Angels were all around helping with the thoughts. Jeshua excused himself as someone really needed help. I found myself falling through this floor of bubbles without him, but then he was back to support me.

It was not a heavy atmosphere. Each prayer and request was looked at and answered in the manner that was best for each individual. All prayers are answered with caring love.

Nile River

About this same time, Jeshua took me on another sojourn. We have all wondered about his hidden years. Part of that time was spent in Egypt. Alexandria at that time was the known spiritual capital to that part of the world. This can be compared to Rome, MECCA, and Jerusalem, as they are known as spiritual capitals today. The Essenes, a Jewish group that his mother belonged to, had a large-size settlement there. Today in our schools we have gifted and talented programs for the outstanding students. It was no different then, as Jesus in the temple displayed his advanced knowledge. After learning all he could from the Jerusalem rabbis, he was sent to the spiritual center, Alexandria, to study.

This sojourn I had was in Egypt, during Jeshua's time. We were as twentieth century visitors back to this Egyptian time period. I was shown from above, a passenger barge on the Nile River. It was a nice barge and decorated a little, although unpainted [no paint in those days]. Jeshua and I were sitting in front, discussing things. He said his teachers in Egypt occasionally used the barge for the students to give them some recreation and a break from their studies. Also some of the boys got homesick now and then, and this outing was to help that also.

He and I finished our discussion and turned to go further back into the barge. There I met his school buddies. They said their names but I begged off of trying to remember names. I'm bad enough with American names, not to mention Jewish or Arabic. Jeshua and I were adults but the boys were twelve, thirteen, fourteen, and fifteen years of age. There were maybe eight of them and they were a happy, smiling group. We stood in a circle and they assured me that Jeshua was the star of their group. We had a good time and did some kidding, and a little verbal teasing as kids at that age do.

When I came out of this scene, that's when the awe and astonishment set in. I tried to refrain from being awestruck too much because I wanted to keep this balanced. I wanted to keep it as friends. I mean, look at whom I'm having these excursions with!

One time Jeshua asked me what I thought of him. I answered that I felt he was a being of love, and I believe this answer pleased him. When I came out of it, I thought, *How can I have an answer so immediate and without a doubt?* I believe it was my higher self that was so quick with these answers. However, it was a true and a good answer. We all have a higher self that stays in the heavenly realm but still helps us on earth whether we realize it or not. Intuition is part of it.

An afterthought: if Jeshua wasn't a being of love, kindness, gentleness, and patience, I would be afraid to converse with him as I do. He would not be the Jeshua that we know if he misused his power. God would not be the God we know if he misused his power. Man makes fear because we deliberately or inadvertently misuse our power in actions, words, or thoughts. We need to come back to love.

The Father

Somewhere I read that Jeshua would lead all to the Father. To me, at this time, the Father is someone up there that we are suppose to love but I know he's all powerful and I'm a little scared and intimidated by the thought of him. After all, they say, "Fear the Lord." Why don't they just say, "Love the Lord?" I understand now that it was the incorrect teachings about a revengeful and angry God that made me feel that way. We attach our human emotions to God and believe he is made up of that. He is above all that—he is just love.

At different times, Jeshua asked me to pray with him, to go to the Father and do it. Finally after the second or third asking, I agreed on the condition that my trust in Jeshua wouldn't be betrayed and, most important, he said he'd do all the talking.

We went to a space and just stood, and Jeshua prayed. God is in nothingness also, so God must have been in this empty space. It worked out very well. After that, at different times Jeshua encouraged me to say a few words to the Father. He is very good at nudging, like saying, "Just give it a little try."

Little by little I did this, as long as Jeshua was there to support me. Slowly my anxiousness disappeared and now it is just fine. But remember, prayer should be like a conversation, it's a two-way affair and your answers can come in many ways. After a year and a half I found myself talking as much to the Father as I did to Jeshua. I won't forget the first couple of times the Father actually talked with me. I was so surprised, it works!

I have read in books of the different names God is called. There's God, Great Spirit, Allah, Jehovah, creator source, and the angels called him the universal conscious, and so on. So I asked, "What do you really want to be called?"

I wasn't expecting an answer, but clear as a bell in my head I heard, *"Call me love."*

I was startled to hear this answer, but I liked it. If you think about it, how many songs do we have about love? They abound; we are all drawn to love. I will take this a step farther and say we are drawn to God, who is in love with all of us. At times you hear that we are all one. Now Jesus says we are love; each love is individual but this is what we are. That means if we are all one by love and God is this love, we're a chip off the old block. I'm not trying to make any theological statement, just simple logic in my mind. We need to respect that gift of love and oneness in ourselves and ourselves. It's our spiritual "DNA."

November 1999

Sunday. This morning on waking, I wanted to, and did, connect with Jeshua. I found him dressed in a purple robe and sitting attentively in a square, modern, deep purple chair. There was a slender black rod in his right hand. There was a small, thin, black matching crown on, of similar material, on his head.

I was off to his right in front of him. Always we greet each other. This time there was no greeting, no eyes meeting, and no acknowledgment. He seemed to be concentrating on something straight ahead of him. From my angle, I couldn't see what he was looking at. I waited for him to finish his task, but that didn't seem to be happening. I started thinking I should go back.

He motioned with his left hand for me to stand behind him. He seemed to be alone but I know there were angels there. I stood behind his left shoulder and now saw what he was concentrating on. About five feet or so apart, there was a path with flat borders. Outside the borders there was nothing. Inside were little lights scattered here and there in clumps or by themselves and more Christmas-like lights twinkled on. This carpet runner of twinkling lights extended on and on. I stayed for awhile observing this and wondering. There still was no conversation and so I left.

I got to church that Sunday morning and found out it was the Catholic day of Christ the King. No wonder the purple color, that's for a king and also the color for high spirituality.

I believe the carpet runner of lights I saw were earthly souls, churches, communities, nations, ultimately the world, and how they were applying his words or thoughts to their lives, etc. The ones that were applying were getting the light of awakening. It was those applying love to the world and living as God would want them to. They were acknowledging God then or the light of God in their lives.

This contact and conversing has become natural to me. I can talk back and forth using mental telepathy with the heavenly world. Really, I mainly converse with Jeshua and the angels, but I've also conversed with Archangel Michael and St. Germain a few times now.

444 January 2000

I discovered that some numbers have certain distinctions about them. 444 is one of them. It signifies that God loves you and the angels are also supporting you. Many people have stories concerning the moments they first notice 444. However I noticed I never received any 444s.

I asked the angels about it and the first time they said I didn't need one. A second time I asked and they said I didn't need it because I could feel the angels and Jeshua close by. Although events are planned in our lives in the world, things can change when we use our thoughts, intentions, or prayers to do so. As I mentioned before, each prayer is answered, so basically I regarded my request for a 444 as something I wasn't going to be able to obtain. However, in January I woke up, looked at the clock and there it was, 4:44. I liked that and fell back into a snug, happy sleep, knowing of God's and the angels' support and love.

Before that day was over I really needed that love and support. At work I was called into the office and found out that my job was not going to be renewed. I was completely surprised and not expecting this blow. Now I really needed some heavenly support. It is said that all things are planned and there are no coincidences. But this was not something I had consciously planned. Where is this leading?

Your first 444 there are no coincidences. It was meant to be this way.

-J

I leaned heavily on the heavenly side at this announcement from the office. The statements below contain more of what Jeshua said to me, as at times I was feeling very down about this.

I see the core of who you are. It is not the educational level or achievement that you attain, but who you are. Come walk with me, the best is yet to be. If I, the savior of the world can say that to you, do not let the measurements of you by others bother you. You are a beautiful person to me; that will never change.

Love J

How absolutely nice and soothing! This could be said for all of us. I was comforted for a while but then it started bothering me again. I needed more support at times to get through this. Here are more uplifting, supporting, and loving words I received from time to time during this situation. Maybe you'll find yourself in such a situation and these words might help you too. These words are from Jeshua relating to this.

Let me be the strong one in this trial.

Don't be afraid. There will have to be changes to be able to do my work. I will put you in the arms of those who are loving and caring about you, to help you. Don't be afraid.

Think of happy times and be comforted. The happy times will return and continue. You remember; they have in your past. I am here.

We are helping you even though you don't know it. We are with you, have confidence. It'll all be okay. We have happy things planned for you.

Trust me, although it may not seem like it, he [God] has provided for you [referring to the future].

My arms are here to come to.

Everything in the world my Father has provided with love. The unpleasant parts planned while a person is in heaven, before being born, they have agreed upon. Earth is a short sojourn, a time for soul development. They [the souls] regain heaven after this sojourn and all that it [earth] offered, for further soul development.. [In heaven] A regained happiness is theirs and gratefulness for their earthly journey with the opportunity to praise God on all levels.

Take heart, things are moving in the universe for you. Take your love then, use it to reestablish [regain balance]. I have seen your sadness and bewilderment. What are you to learn from this? Love my dear, no matter what the situation. Trust my dear, of our help. Faith my dear, we are always near, as is God's presence even though you think it is a mystery. I enjoy you coming to me—as you enjoy—in joy. See there is happiness in our communication.

In joy, let this continue and perpetuate—let that continue in your ever present moment.

At the time, I looked at the above statements and thought Wow! I never was into religion or spirituality that much and to write this way was something else. It was all from above and all very good to me. This event also fit in with one of the Shaumbra Symptoms, a sudden loss of job or career.

I survived that surprise and in hindsight saw where this worked in my lifetime. With a full-time job, there is no time really to read and research this material. Now I had time to do this and I took advantage of it, because learning and new outlooks have occurred for me.

Pets and Reunions

Like many, I have had favorite animals that have been pets. We feel very bad when their time comes to go, and we may wonder what, if anything, will happen to them. The following I hope will answer that question and set your mind at ease. This episode I recall fondly.

Jeshua said, "Let's go to heaven." I said, "Okay."

First he introduced me to the apostles. I could see human forms but not the faces. They were casually lined up facing us. I was rather bashful and stood a little behind Jeshua. He grinned at my bashfulness. I did a general hello because I didn't know what name went with what form or what to say. To add to my embarrassment I didn't remember all their names anyhow.

Next we meet Verna. She was a friend I shared a passion for horses with. Unfortunately she died in a car accident in her twenties many years ago. It was arranged between us before this happened that if anything happened to her, she wanted me to have her horse, Gaylon. So, through her generosity I received Gaylon. I had her for nineteen years, and just about three generations of my family were able to ride her. She passed away at almost thirty-six years of age, which is very old for a horse.

I told Verna how Gaylon was doing, that her systems were slowly shutting down and she was getting into rough shape.

Verna knew this though and told me that Gaylon wouldn't last long.

Next my parents came together to see me. I thank them for the most important things they've done for me during my life. I'm not surprised at seeing them because I believe that we all go to heaven for reunion. I thank my dad for being a farmer. This instilled in me the love of nature, animals and the outdoors. For my mother, I thanked her for her strong religious insistence. That is sure helping out now.

I can't forget my ex-husband's folks who I came to love. They came to me together and again I thank them for the most important things they did in my life. I thanked my father-in law for his sense of humor even while seeing into the core of a problem. I thanked my mother-in-law for her unconditional acceptance and love of who I was.

Horses

Next Jeshua came leading my two horses from my youth, Trixie and Loafin, who had passed on. These were the two horses I had in my teen years and twenties. I was so very surprised; I wasn't expecting this and was very happy to see them. I could even feel tears of happiness rolling down my face. I went up to them and just looked, petted, and spoke to them.

Jeshua said, "Let's go for a ride," so I give him Loafin as he's taller. Then I start warning Jeshua that Loafin's afraid of wires that are down on the ground from fences, so be on the lookout for that, because he might shy away. Then I caught myself thinking, *Why am I saying that? There are no down fences in heaven.*

On our ride in heaven we galloped, like on clouds, bareback with just a halter and a rope. The horses behaved beautifully and Jeshua was a good rider. I was sure to assess his skills for bareback riding. There was no need to worry, and he was enjoying this thoroughly. I can still see him with a delighted smile on his face, wind blowing his hair back, and robes a flying. That would be a good picture for horse people. He has blue eyes that you'd remember.

Pretty soon we stopped—it was a hillside where we could see through the young trees. After slowing to a walk we rode through the trees and then dismounted. I was concerned about tying up the horses, but Jeshua said "They're okay and will eventually find their way back to their heavenly home."

Through the trees we could see a green meadow with long grass and a clear stream. We sat down and looked for wildlife while we visited. On the humorous side, on these visits there are no mosquitoes! There are benefits of horseback riding in your dreams.

Not much later, on another night, we took another ride with the horses. We were striding through space. I looked down at the blackness with stars and thought, *Space shuttles go faster than this; it'll take forever at a horse's walk.* Sometimes I think of the darnest things in dreams.

This ride ended with a picture I will always carry in my heart. I was in front, facing the horses. On my left was Loafn's head and body, and on the right was Trixie's head and body. Just above that in the center—leaning down from the horses back—was Jeshua's smiling face. I drew a heart around all of this. It was almost Valentine's Day and he sure knows how to give a good Valentine gift. Really these are the three that meant a lot to me in my growing up teen and young- adult years.

Just a side note about my old mare Gaylon, who I eventually lost. I knew she was going because of her poor health, I just didn't know when. All of my family felt bad when she passed on and, when she was gone, I asked Jeshua if he could bring Gaylon's spirit to me. Sure enough in a dream, Jeshua was standing there sideways and in the distance I saw a figure. It came trotting towards him, and I recognized it was my old mare. She trotted up to Jeshua and stood by him. He put his hand on her and smiled. She was now healthy and happy with a shiny coat, and her long mane and tail beautifully groomed. How nice he did that for me as it gave me much comfort to see her again. She was such a sweet mare. So when there are pets we were very fond of that pass on, it's nice to know we will meet them on the other side. There they are in good health and of course younger. I've heard the same goes with people when they pass over. If they are to look like their body, it most likely will be in their younger years. They get to choose which age (usually the twenties or thirties) they want to stay in. Also we can then also choose whether to be male or female.

Second Past Life

I'm who? I'm what? St. Rita

I had no idea the following story was coming, but come it did. You would think a person would get used to this, but then a corner is turned and another surprise comes. In meditation in the family room, about February, Jeshua and I were visiting. We don't need physical words for me to know it is him, the awareness just comes interiorly, mentally. It's all done with his energy and can come so fast and be so clear. This was a short but very strong meditation.

Jeshua told me of a person I was in a past lifetime. He told me her name was Rita, she was a nun. She was a saint who lived in the thirteenth or fourteenth century. I was thinking, *He doesn't know whether it's the thirteenth or the fourteenth century she lived in, so maybe there's no validity to this.* I didn't feel I was ready to struggle with another past life revelation. I humored myself at the idea I was a nun without even getting to the saint part. I got up to leave him in the room as I didn't want to accept this, especially this kind of life. Before I left the room though, Jeshua gave me a quick glimpse of a nun in black, kneeling before him.

I was reluctant about going to my small-town library to see if I could find anything on her. That last lifetime description had been a biggie, I wasn't sure I wanted to go into this again. However I was really curious and Jeshua knew that. I didn't know anything about her and I was half hoping I wouldn't find anything. *This is a figment of my imagination right?*

But that Jeshua sure can make life interesting. After turning this around in my mind for a couple of days, I did go to our town library. I was curious and I wanted to find out if I could validate this. The small library had just two books on saints. I reached up and took one book off the shelf. Opening it, I didn't see a Rita listed in it and I let out a long sigh of relief. I reached up, got the other book, opened it, and there she was. I read the short description and caught my breath. I read it again. It was practically word-for-word as Jeshua had told me with maybe a sentence or two more. I stared at that and reread it again. Everything around the perimeter of the book became blurry as I continued to stare and try to comprehend how everything Jeshua told me about her was exactly as printed in the book—almost word-for-word. All four items were correct. My hope that thirteenth and fourteenth century dates where a mix-up and would make this whole thing invalid was quickly put to rest. Sr. Rita was born in the thirteenth century and died in the fourteenth century.

> My reaction? *Me, a former saint! I'm not telling anyone this. They'll really think I'm goofy, but really I'm not. I'm just having these extraordinary experiences. Everything Jeshua told me has come out true! I started to struggle and grope with this revelation. Suddenly I began having an identity crisis. Who am I? I thought of the book, The Power of Now. Really, this is who I am, this present now. The past is the past and the future is to come, we just have this now.*

That thought gave me some comfort and resolution.

In both these revelations of past lives, Jeshua gave me something to relate to in my present physical world to help me believe what he had told me. The first lifetime was the unannounced flood of tears, and now this accurate description. I knew nothing about Sr. Rita or had any idea about her life. My motto of expecting the unusual as usual was being used again.

I started researching. I wanted to find out more about her. I purchased a couple of books about her from the Internet. I was fascinated to begin reading, and also afraid of what I'd find. Yet I had to find out, this was getting good, and led to another intriguing adventure.

Briefly I'll tell you about her. Rita was the only child born to an older couple in Italy. Her father was a sheep farmer and the local mediator for the area neighborhood disputes.

This was a very disturbing time politically for that area in Italy. As a baby her mother put her in a basket while she tended the garden. When she checked on her there were bees crawling in and out of her mouth. There was not any harm being done to the baby but this caused much wonderment in the neighborhood.

From an early age, Rita showed signs of a love for Jeshua. When she was fourteen years old her parents wanted her to marry. She resisted for quite a while as she wanted to go into the convent, but in the end she obeyed their wishes. She was married for eighteen years and had two sons, twins. Her husband was abusive. A couple of years before her husband died, Rita was able to turn his behavior around and he became a loving man. Within a short time both her parents died and her husband was murdered. That left her to raise her teenage sons who wanted revenge for the murder of their father. However, she believed in forgiveness and would sooner have them die than have them take revenge by killing. Within a year both of her boys died of other causes but not before they learned how to forgive.

Alone at the age of thirty-six, Rita was free to enter the convent. All through her life she had practiced devotions and developed a spiritual life. The convent wouldn't take her though, for one or both of the following reasons. She was a widow and had been married. And secondly, her husband's relatives and some of the convent sisters had relatives in the community that were at odds with Rita's in-laws. Rita tried to have peace made in these relationships and this was eventually accomplished, written up, and signed on paper. However she was still denied entrance to the convent. After three or so tries she received heavenly aid and was accepted into the convent. In her new life, she turned out to be a very prayerful soul with the strongest devotion to Jeshua, especially toward his passion and death. After fifteen years in the convent, Jeshua gave her a stigma of a thorn on the forehead. Stigmata are wounds that occur about the same places as Jeshua's crucifixion wounds were. For the person receiving these wounds, they don't heal and some get all five of them. Rita only got one. A few individuals have had this phenomenon; and for Rita this one included a foul odor with it, which also didn't heal. This made it difficult for others to be around her and resulted in her being left alone much of the time. A few miracles were now being accorded to her. There were things like a dead twig turning into a flowering vine, and picking roses and figs in the middle of the winter from her former garden. She was talking back and forth to the heavenly world but none of the conversations were written down. Toward the end of her life, Rita had been ill for some time. The day before she died, Jeshua and Mary appeared to her to say she was coming home. She said, "At last," meaning she was ready. The bells rang in the church steeple at the exact time of her passing, and the nuns looked at each other, knowing no one had given any order for that to be done.

Since Rita was known in the community, the nuns thought there would be a notable funeral and then life would continue on normally. This was not to be the case. Rita's body became incorruptible with the smell of roses coming from it. Her incorrupt body is still in Italy 600 years later. Again, I wouldn't have known anything about this unless Jeshua had told me about it, and the books I found on her. After reading about her life and her times I guess I wouldn't blame her for wanting to be a nun and becoming one. She had an immense devotion for Jeshua that I now understand.

About four years after all this started for me, I was going through old papers I had kept; they were probably eight years old or so. To my surprise I came upon a prayer card for St. Rita. I remember thinking at the time I first got it, This is *another saint being promoted,* and I was going to throw it out. However I noted that she was the saint for "the impossible" and thought, *I might need that sometime,* and I kept the prayer card. I did not use it but how ironic!

In 2008 I was privileged to go to Cascia, Italy, and Rocpuccinera, Rita's hometown and church. She was raised by her parents in Rocpuccinera and lived her married life there. Those two small towns are three miles apart, and it's an easy downhill walk back to Cascia. Near the end of this walk my companions and I were on, and before we got to Cascia, Rita's parents came to me. Her mother had the widest beaming smile and projected her love to me. I now know why her father was well known in the area to be a moderator. As he conversed with me, I sensed his keen mind and the ability to articulate very well his clear thoughts. The main thing I remembered out of the conversation I had with him is "Remember what we taught you, to love God with all your heart."

A couple of years before I went to Italy, I had asked Jeshua to take me there. In a dream or vision, we ended up by the cross that is painted on the wall at the convent. This is where I believe Rita received her stigma. Jeshua was standing to one side of the painted cross and I was on the other. We were facing each other. The twentieth century me was so moved at that time that I wanted to do an all-out, on-the-floor prostration to him. This must have been a Rita part coming through. These sites are open to the public now and being in spirit, no one could see us, but I was afraid someone would still step on me. So I just huddled down close to the wall and did devotion there. The painting is what stood out for me emotionally during the present-day convent tour when I did make it physically to Cascia in 2008.

The church there is very beautiful and I liked its more modern aspects. As I gazed around at the people standing there, all I could think of was, *Remember your own power. Don't give it away. You have it in you.*

Yes, saints and masters are more than willing to help, but it is your responsibility to help yourself develop in spirit. Even the Blessed Virgin in Medjugorje said you have your own internal guide. It can be called intuition, insights, or hunches.

Rita had joined the Augustinian order of nuns. As I sat in the church, I reconnected with St. Rita. I received a strong feeling of the love she had for her order. She's with them now, that's for sure, and aiding those who ask for help the best she can.

Do some of the characteristics or thoughts patterns of who you were before carry over into who and what you are now? Some characteristics you had in past lives do carry over into who you are in this life. To put this in an understandable context, I like to look at these tendencies of past lives, whether good or bad, as the walls of a cylindrical cone. There are no ends at the top or bottom of the cone. Our present life experiences rise up through this cylindrical cone of past life experiences. How many of these experiences on the walls touch us, to help or hinder us, is up to each individual or their higher self to decide. Sometimes it doesn't take much of a touch for a tendency to flower. Don't we all know someone who has a real talent or something similar and we wonder where they got it from?

So what about me, now that I was supposed to be this person? What were these tendencies? Has my relation to Jeshua increased as a result of all this? Immensely! I never would have dreamed up any of this. How can you not have a good relationship with him? For me it's close. For Rita it was close. She was able to talk to Jeshua, God, and others on the heavenly side. This is occurring for me now. Rita had a devotion to Jeshua, especially concerning his passion. That pattern of the stoning, during his passion, is where I was introduced to all of this. Miriam was pricked on her forehead by a thorn, and Rita received a thorn stigma in the same area. There are prayer cards picturing her with a beam of light streaming at her forehead, and I've had that happen to me two or three times. It feels like I'm getting a computer download. This started in her fifties—about the same age all this occurred with me. Miriam, Rita and myself each like rural areas and lived in them. Rita didn't write any important dogma or start an order, and the church never could figure out why she was liked so well through time. One reason could be the type of marriage and family life she had. In the fifteenth century, a bishop in Spain called her "the saint of the impossible," that could be another reason. She wasn't canonized (when the Catholic Church officially makes a person a saint) until five hundred years after her death. The exterior signs of starting an order or writing a great thesis are not necessary for sainthood. Everything starts and is from the heart, and finding and living from that. I believe there are many, many silent saints today and in times past that haven't been acknowledged.

All of us have had past lifetimes, reincarnations. Our reincarnated lives are well planned before we come here to learn or complete a lesson that was needed and/or maybe to help others with their lessons. It is fascinating to me to see how this is unfolding. If Rita knew of her life in Jeshua's time, I'm not sure, but devotion to him she did know.

We, in the Western hemisphere, are starting to discover reincarnation. Each of us has had many past lives. The knowledge we gained in each life is still contained in our higher self or soul on the other side. This is a great store of knowledge that is there for us to tap into. We just have to relearn, to be reminded how to tap into it again, by going within. This can be done with meditation, intuition, or contemplation, minus the mind and ego. It is a boost of confidence to know we have this knowledge as a backup along with angels and other heavenly beings that aid us with their guidance.

In pondering and realizing this, my mind goes, "Who am I?" Me in this present day wins out. The truth is, we should only live our present lives. That's all we have. Yesterday is gone and tomorrow is still to come. By realizing our yesterdays and learning from them, it will help us to live our todays better. Our tomorrows are the result of our todays. We are all on our own individual paths of self-responsibility to help others and ourselves in our spiritual evolution by setting our positive intentions and carrying them out.

Being that I was able to find information on Rita, there have not been very many dreams or visions that have come to me. The only thing I can remember is an arched wall that was a corridor along the outside wall of a building.

St. Rita's garden

My relationship with Jeshua now ranges from just being together and not communicating, to humor with wordplay, to conversation and informational discussions, and at times, devotion. The following was one of those conversational times.

Previously I mentioned Jeshua asked me what color I wanted my house. I had no idea why he asked that. Below is the start of how that came about.

In a vision we went to a beautiful garden. There were wide white steps up a small slope with beautiful white, pink, and violet blossoms on either side. He and I picked some of the blossoms and threw them up in the air to praise and thank God. What was nice was that the blossoms came down to where they were before still as beautiful and perfuse as ever.

Two days later I was typing about the stoning for this book, when the following happened. I felt I had come to a resolution about my feelings regarding the stoning, but typing about it brought some of the emotions to the forefront again. I was starting to feel bad and Jeshua knew this and came to me. We went to the garden again, sat on the top step and he consoled me. In a bit I was smiling again and feeling a lot better. The book *Course in Miracles*, talks about how we can resolve some things temporarily, but we can revert and need to get balanced again. I felt healed after the wound presentation, but after a while I brought back up some of the same emotions again, so Jeshua came back to help me through them again.

After this, we walked further into the garden and came to a small white fountain like a bird bath with a small jet of water sprouting from the middle. Jesus was saying how water is the life of the earth in everything that it reaches. He continued, *"Let's say this fountain is love."*

I say, "Like the violet flame or color which can also symbolize love or can transform our emotions and thoughts." The small jet of water turned a lovely shade of violet, slowly turning the rest of the fountain water the same shade. This time though it spilled from the fluted edges around the fountain and the purple water went in all directions from the fountain.

> Jeshua said, *"This is God's love for all, for us humans and his creations. It is life giving, it flows in all directions, and is never ending"*

What a beautiful thought. We can do our part to keep it flowing by practicing forgiveness and love every day.

Jeshua then handed me some prayer requests. I thought of the prayer vine I'm in and so I asked God to help them and I handed it over to God. Then Jeshua handed me a lot more requests, fresh ones. I was puzzled, but then I had a thought. I often wondered who took over the prayer requests of St Rita if in fact she is reincarnated here on earth now. I decided it must be her higher self, so I handed them over to her.

We are composed of four different parts. In the physical we are composed of body, mind, and emotions. But who can put their hands out and physically hand us their spirit, soul, or their higher self? It can be talked about but not handed to you. Our higher selves are in another dimension and are yet still with us, guiding us while we are in our physical form. When we leave our physical form, emotions, and mind on earth when we die, we then go to the heavenly dimension of our spirit, soul, and higher self that is and was always there.

Jeshua now handed me a huge, older volume of requests compared to the other ones. What can I do? I'm beginning to feel like a swamped person with a desk piled two feet high with work spilling over onto the floor. I asked God's help for them, prayed, and handed them over to God. I am not at all sure how this really works, but it is how it worked that morning. God is the ultimate problem solver. As we pray to him, we should also pray for each other and ask for one another's help and blessings. Our prayers can be so powerful, it is even better when we do it correctly. That is explained later on.. I also like the saying, Let go and let God.

Spring of 2000

I was beginning to accept all of this a little more by now, but then one day I took stock. I understand that I'm supposed to write my story. In this story I'm supposed to acknowledge that I can converse back and forth with the heavenly side. I'm to acknowledge that I can talk with Jeshua; and, not only that, I knew him during his life on earth.

I decided, *Gal, you have a problem.*

In my head came the reply, "What problem?"

Now that was not the backup I was looking for. After a while I decided, Well, if Jeshua doesn't have a problem with this, I won't either. I'm trusting that love.

So I was good for a little while with this settlement in my mind but…there it started again, AC alternating consciousness. This bothered me and I really wanted to get to the bottom of this.

In this episode, Jeshua and I were together in a gray area, or clouds. He was about four feet away, standing still. I started walking a circle around him and he turned in the center of the circle, facing me as I walked. I stopped and questioned, "You want me to believe all this?"

After a pause and no answer from him, I continued walking my circle. Again I stopped and asked, "You want me to tell others of this?"

Again there was no answer, he just looked at me. From all those experiences he gave me, the answer has to come from deep within myself. That was his silent answer to me.

So, today, my ultimate answer, in light of the times we are living in, is to help people evolve spiritually and realize these truths.

Reeling

Later on I purchased some angel cards. I thought it'd be fun to use, being they were very positive messages. The cards depicted an angel with a word stating an explanation of the pose that each angel was conveying. The process was to put three cards face down, and turn them over to see the pictures and words. I had a certain question to ask. But the angels had a different question they wanted me to ask. The question they wanted me to ask was how I could love Jeshua more.

I still persisted with my question and they persisted with theirs. So I said "okay" to the angels, thinking I'd get back to my original question sooner or later. So my question was changed to "How could I love Jeshua more?"

After the question was asked, I started to draw a card. The angels just wanted one card drawn, which was unusual, but I said "Okay."

I drew one card, which was face down. Then I turned it over and the word on it was: soul mate. My mind reeled; my world spun as I thought of my question and the card I received. At that moment I felt one of those huge bursts of love from Jeshua and the angels. *Wow, this love does more than sweep you off your feet.*

I must say, that feeling stayed with me for a few days after that. Then I started searching for information. There had to be more to the meaning of soul mate than I was thinking of. To my relief, I found a definition of soul mate as one who comes into your life for an important event, or to work through karma. The karma can even be an unpleasant or pleasant one. There definitely was pleasant karma in this relationship.

> Even the angels knew how stunned I could be by this, let alone trying to believe it. So they gave me extra encouragement shortly after the above happened. After I was completing a calming meditation in a pastoral setting, I heard, *"Rest your mind, heart, and soul in this tranquility. Cherish it and REMEMBER it, so these doubts no longer assail you. You know these conversations are true now. Recall this truth, this tranquility of knowing, so this can be put to rest and you can move forward."*
>
> *-Your angels.*

The angels' explanations were a lot more clear than anything I could think of, so I accepted that.

There came a point in time when I had to decide how to be friends with Jeshua. Here was someone that lived two thousand years ago, affected millions of lives worldwide over time, and changed the course of history. At times I was really undecided on how to handle this. He came and told me to just work with him as a man. This I do, but I also remember that he is an exceptional, extraordinary man. From that angle I was able to handle things better, but I also remember his divinity too, he was a man who was Christed. He relates to us on our own levels of thinking and personality, and that makes it so much easier for us to relate to him. He is love personified.

There is much love and respect on my part also for Jeshua. The book *Course in Miracles* states that we are all one; we are all brothers, including him. He acknowledges, though, at the beginning of the book, that we respect him so much because he is much more experienced than us. There have been times when I am so moved I would say, "your servant," or be submissive and want to kneel. Yet each time he answered me in the same manner to that comment, that a servant is not needed. At any inclination of my kneeling and he would raise me up to my feet. It's as if to reinforce his statement that he is like us.

> *In God's light, neither [him or us] are servant in your sense of the word but we gratefully acknowledge God in us and know that.*
>
> -J

Like the chat rooms on the Internet, I've decided I have a chat room with heaven. I'll talk with him or the angels throughout the day (talk is prayer), take the time to meditate (meditation is listening) and visit. We can all have our own heavenly chat room.

I believe if there were nicknames in that realm, they might call me a chatterbox at times. This is the direct opposite of what I really am in person. Rather than saying memorized prayers, it's chatting back and forth with the heavenliest, which is great. I definitely have changed my mind of how prayer could be.

There have been times for me where it is uncanny how things work out. As I got more into this, I found I like to meditate by myself so there were no distractions. Sometimes I have the problem of how can I get my husband out of the house so I can do this. Well, the heavenly side will want to visit with me too, and soon the telephone will ring and he will need to go somewhere. Okay, that's fine, it works for me. I now have the house to myself for a heavenly visit. They say there are no coincidences

Episode II

DIMENSIONAL TRAVEL

There have been other episodes, maybe not as moving to me but still nice to recall. We haven't gone into the future, just the present or the past. Usually I'm shown a general scene from above, so I know where we are, and then we go into it. Below are a few.

Reacquainting Party

One time Jeshua wanted me to go to heaven with him to meet my angels. Well, I got a feeling we were standing there and these angels went by saying their names. I begged off, trying to remember names and the angels said, "You don't remember us, but we remember you. We are friends and you give a humorous, joyful curve to life."

Okay, I was game, and so the angels and I got reacquainted. Jeshua stood to the side, grinning and enjoying the happy reacquainting party.

Greece

In another trip I was shown beautiful white buildings on top of different hills. They were very white and noticeable from a distance. This was Athens, Greece, in the distant past, when the Acropolis, etc., were in their original forms.

Jeshua and I were on a roof of a building toward the front, looking down. On the wide steps going into the building were a group of men dressed in robes of Greek garb of that time. There was someone on the top step of the group talking to them.

Jeshua said that this was Socrates, his friend.

> I listened in. Socrates is saying *unless we acknowledge a higher being, then we are making ourselves lower than we need to be.*

To me Socrates message meant that we are to acknowledge God above us, around us, and within us. If we sincerely do that, then we will think, speak, and act appropriately to the glorious self that is in us. It will spill over in our actions to our brothers, ourselves, and the environment; and the whole world will be a better place. Individually and together all need to do this for evolvement and for betterment to happen.

After the above occurred, I read that Socrates felt there was someone or something guiding him in his life. I wondered if that was Jeshua, among other guides, considering what he had just showed and told me.

I want to say a couple of words here on angels and guides. We all know we have guardian angels with us. There are two, sometimes more, and they can change depending on what stage of life we are in or what we have going on in our lives. Besides this there is also a guide. This could be a relative that died long before we were born, but they need to have training in order to be a guide. They always have to respect our free will and can guide us, but not tell us what to do. Besides this, there is the Holy Spirit, highly evolved souls like Jeshua, and God to guide us.

India

On this trip, there was no conversation, no ideas presented, just a trip. I was shown from above a row among other rows of small square huts that I thought were homes. They were painted white, and some had rusty metal roofs with dirt streets between them. It was early morning in India, present day. I don't remember seeing people present but after this view we sat on a dome. We just sat and looked at the eastern horizon. I remember thinking about slipping off and I promised myself, on another trip like this I'll take along an invisible deer tree stand so I won't slip. We looked at the horizon and I noticed the morning mist in the distance. There was no conversation and that was the end of it.

Why did Jesus take me to India? There has been speculation that perhaps Jesus made a trip to India during his life. I bet he did; why would we go there otherwise? Was this his way of showing me? Maybe he just wanted to remember and think.

I present a new concept of again thinking outside the box. Man has put God in a box by using our concepts to understand him. Jeshua came and tried at that time 2,000 years ago to help others think outside the box about God. One time I asked him if we every stop learning in heaven. His answer—*"Is God limited?"* explains it all. So let's try to think outside the box we put Jesus in. We have guardian angels and before I spoke of guides. Now we'll agree that Jeshua had angels to help him, and also (I believe) guides. In India, the Hindu religion has been around five thousand years or more. They have highly regarded saints and people who were absolutely noted for their spirituality. One of these distinguished persons is called Krishna. In *Autobiography of a Yoga* by Paramahansa Yogananda, I read that Krishna and Jeshua are friends on the higher realm. Krishna brought spiritual concepts to India, and Jeshua did the same for Israel and the West. (Maybe that was an additional reason why we went to India). We went to India because he had a trip in that region 2,000 years ago. If so, did he bring some of their concepts or practices back with him? I understand there are some concepts in Tibetan religion that are on the same order as Christianity. This is just my musings, but it's interesting to think about. Our world might be a lot smaller than we think it is, our religions having universal truths and concepts in them. There are many good but different paths to God, and all should be honored. However the main path is from our hearts.

Dolphins

Christmas and New Year's of 2000 presented another fun time. A few nights before, I had looked at a *National Geographic* article on dolphins and thought it would be fun to swim with them. I didn't see that happening anytime soon, but in another way it did.

In this event I saw the white sand, clear blue water, gentle lapping waves. It was a beach in a tropical place, but I don't know where. Jeshua and I had the place to ourselves and of course I was aware that angels were around. I didn't see them but I knew they were there.

There were two white beach lounging chairs close to the waterline, which were reclining, high back, wooden chairs. We sat down for just a short time, visited, and then he called my attention to dolphins swimming out in the water. He asked if I want to go swimming with them. Of course I want to go, but I'm not sure how. He said he'd show me.

So we were out there and he was showing me how to hang on. He stayed with me until I had enough confidence, and then I said, "I want to do it myself."

So Jeshua gets on the other dolphin and we go through the water. It's fun, real easy, and nothing scary. He went his way and

I decided I wanted to get off to see if the dolphins would bump into me to keep me a float. That's just what they did! It's neat.

Soon I noticed Jeshua was back on the beach chair and I decided to go back also. Before I walked back through the water to the beach, I turned to look at the dolphin. I still can see it as plain as if this happened today. The dolphin's right eye was by me, maybe three feet away. I could see its coloring, eyelid, and he telepathically says to me, "You know, you have the savior of the world with you."

I simply said, "Yes, I know," and then turn and go back to the beach to where Jeshua is waiting.

Third Past Life

Egypt – Suspicions, Questions

Just when we leave this world the one big thing we take with us is love and the learned lessons of our soul experience. How well have we loved? Jeshua comments on this follows.

> *Our legacy lives on in love, whether in past lives, present, or the future. Remember that.*
>
> *It's a past that affects our present of how we feel, think, are.*
>
> *Love reaches across the ages to be known and felt again.*

How do I begin the next lifetime? Again an answer is told to me in such a way so that if I believe what is happening to me in the present, then this other is true also. I'm at the point now where I have had so much given to me, that I now say, "Bring it on." What else could there be? I can't be anymore flabbergasted than I have already been.

Even though I have had these excursions with Jeshua, I can't help but think, *What is this?* Usually you hear about Jeshua appearing to someone, giving love, stating something important and that's it. Here I am going on horseback rides with him, swimming with dolphins, dancing, visiting countries in various timeframes. This just isn't matching up very well in my thinking as I turn this over and over in my mind. Although I enjoyed the experiences, I am left wondering, Why he would initiate such things as these? I try to think of reasons why, but the reasons are not strong enough because the questioning in my mind starts again. I can't figure it out.

When I was doing research about the 2,000-years-ago incident in Edgar Cayce's "Story of Jeshua," he said that Jeshua had a few reincarnations before he became Jeshua. According to Cayce, Jeshua's important incarnations in the world's history are "Amilius, Adam, Melchiezdek, Zend, Ur, Asaph, Jeshua, Joseph, (Joshua) Jeshua." Keep this in mind for the following lifetime description.

While still at my previous job, my assistant videotaped the musical, *Joseph and the Technicolor Dream Coat*. I asked her if I could watch it as I liked the musical and hadn't seen it in a while. Soon I was reading in the Bible about Joseph. I ran across the sentence that he was married to the high priest's daughter when he came into the pharaoh's favor. He had two sons with her. The words come across my mind, *I bet I was her*. But then I tell myself, *This is a bunch of c__p,* slammed the book closed, and walked away. *This is ridiculous!* But it did stay in my mind. Advice in a book on psychic phenomenon says don't doubt or dismiss your first impression. *Oh no, what's coming now?*

Sometimes I'm ready for this and sometimes I'm not.

June Horse trip

I have had premonitions, feelings, or views that came true. I think of it as no big deal, we've all had that. I received the following premonitions.

The first premonition: I was leading a group of people on a horse ride in bright sunlight. I turned around to look at them and thought, *Why would I be leading a group?*

The second premonition: I was talking with a strange woman who was sitting and I was standing. And I was thinking, What circumstances would I be talking to a stranger? Well...

My friends and I had been riding our horses on a vacation. During the last part, we trail-rode to a remote bunkhouse for a three-day stay. The first day out of the entire ride, I was leading the group in sunlight and turned around to realize that this was the group I'd had a premonition about. Later, when we were at the bunkhouse the second to last night, I was talking to a new friend. She and her husband had volunteered to be our trail guides. She was sitting; I was standing, and we were visiting with each other. All of a sudden I realized this was the stranger I was talking to in the premonition. Again Jeshua was showing me that what I get in dreams is coming about in my present-day life.

As we were riding, I noticed there were a lot of butterflies at the streams we crossed. No one else made comments about them or seemed to notice them. I admired them though. One night in a dream, Jeshua said he would send me a butterfly. I didn't really seriously consider this dream, but I proved myself wrong. The next day we stopped at a stream to rest and eat lunch. There was a large light-colored butterfly with a small section of its tail torn, but it could still fly very well. It just stayed on this one rock as I approached and it didn't move. I reached toward the butterfly and practically touched it before it flew away. From then on, I have been on the outlook for butterflies for I certainly remember this one. I later learned that sometimes people like to think of butterflies symbols for angels.

That night I dreamt again. I said, "You sent me a butterfly. What next?"

He said he'd send me two deer. I was concerned about the horses getting frightened and shy, as the trails were narrow, hilly, and wooded. I got the reassurance that he and the angels would take care of it.

I was up the next day, wondering about this because all the trails we were riding on were forested. The trails were single file and if a deer came across our path, it would certainly startle the horses. Also if I was at the end of the line I'd never see the deer that crossed over at the beginning of our group of horses.

In deciding on that day's ride, our new friends said there was a lookout over the stable, and we'd go there first. When we got there, we tied the horses to the hitching posts farther back, and walk to the lookout. There was pasture below where the stable was. This was the only opening from the forest surrounding it. As we were looking down, all of a sudden someone said "Look, there are two deer."

Sure enough, there were two deer, not one or three, that walked from the forest into an open area that was easy to see and where the horses wouldn't be startled. All I could think of was what Jeshua said in the dream. He and the angels worked very well together.

So that night, as I was reflecting on things, I said, "What will you send tomorrow?"

An angel replied this time saying, "We'll get you home safe."

Tomorrow we were leaving to for our drive back home, so this reassurance was comforting.

It was that night or the next that this following dream occurred at home.

It was a dark area except for a bright shaft of light coming down. I heard this clink and dragging, like a stone was being dragged across another stone. The shaft of light was gone, and I thought that the Egyptians used to bury some of their people alive. I was thinking if I was in that position I'd take some poison. Then I switched to being that person, and I searched out and found the prepared room for Joseph, and went in. I remember thinking to myself "*I must remember what Joseph told me about his God.*"

Then I returned to present time and chided myself with the thought, "Now look how I'm talking."

Was this a 1700 BC flashback? Sometimes karma from other lifetimes carries over to the present, be it pleasant or unpleasant. It's becoming an accepted fact that drugs and therapy won't work in some circumstances. The need for past-life regression helps to shed light of past events to clear up present life problems, and much more progress is made in the healing of issues.

After this, Jeshua and I were very actively conversing in my sleep. It just seemed like a very steady, fast beam of communication coming from him. I do not remember all that he said because I was searching through his words for the reason for these questionable wonderings I mentioned before. Then he told me this, and I remember because this was the answer to my search. Yes, I was Asaneth, Joseph's wife. When I reacted to him, I was reacting to him as Joseph. After this I just felt it within me, this is true.

I understood now these feelings, these reactions, these experiences I kept turning over and over in my mind and couldn't settle. Now it was settled, I just knew it. I also knew that no other lifetimes would be exposed now. This is it. I told myself, Someone had to be these people, but me? But on the other hand, what a privilege, and honor. This sure could explain the closeness and familiarity I feel to him as he was throughout all these lifetimes.

My other idea was, how appropriate. One thing about Joseph's life was that he was noted for his dreams and interpretations of dreams. And now I was receiving this all in a dream.

Sometimes I get scenes in my mind about this lifetime. The following are these scenes about Egypt. If you need a refresher about Joseph, it's in the old testament of the Bible, Genesis Chapters 37 to 50. In remembering events in this manner or retrogression, you can do it as that person or be an observer. In all these episodes of lifetimes, I've switched back and forth from actually feeling the emotions of that person to just being an observer with none of the emotion involved.

Joseph and Asenath

We started with Asenath, as a young teenager. Of course, she had heard about Joseph, had seen him, and knew others admired him. The circumstances around his finding the Pharaoh's favor were unusual. Her father was an influential man not only in his business/religious affairs but also within his family. He had arranged Asenath's marriage to Joseph. He knew she'd do as he wished; there really wasn't much reason for objection.

Asenath didn't know how well she was going to like this. She had heard a lot of good things said about Joseph, but still he was older, and a stranger to her. Of course, Joseph knew of this apprehension, gave her respect and time, and let the relationship work itself out. This definitely started the marriage on the correct footing. There can be a marriage on the physical, but there can also be a marriage with love, which is so much better. She found him personally to be a very likeable guy on the inside as well as the outside. A year into their marriage, his being older did not matter to her anymore. Love had blossomed and that really helped make it a marriage in the truest sense. It was a very happy, close marriage. The marriage was met on all three levels—the physical, emotional, and with Joseph, definitely the spiritual.

She liked his view of his faith. They had just one God, not the many gods of Egypt. His was less confusing and made more sense. He was so very good at explaining it and helping her understand. Yet, with Asenath, because of her father's position and with what was expected of her in that regard, she had to lean openly to toward the Egyptian religion. What she felt for Joseph's religion, she had to keep to herself.

Later on, I received this: Joseph and Asenath were having evening supper at their living quarters. It must have been early in their marriage as I don't remember any children present. There was a large room, about fifty by thirty-five feet. The floor was smooth, without any carpets. It was sparsely furnished. Any furnishings there were, were around the outer perimeter of the room. Ahead, were windows with about a six- to eight-inch thick tan side wall. There were curtains, like a small sheet gently blowing into the room from the outside breeze. The wall in the front of the room, in the center, had a door with a sentry or guard on the outside. The back wall of the room had the doorway to their bedroom. To the left, about two-thirds of the way down this wall was the doorway to their dining area. I remember the dining room feeling very open like a patio or a covered porch. I believe it was on the roof of a room below where you had to step down to it. There they had their evening meal. It must have been late in the evening because they went through the large open room together to retire to the bedroom. They had to step down to the bedroom. As I watched them walk toward the bedroom, I heard that this was the night their child was conceived.

Before waking one morning this came to me: Again, Jeshua was talking to me, fast, like a light beam of words. I know I liked what I was hearing but don't remember any of it but the following. These words flowed through me as it was Asenath speaking. "Joseph and Asenath—their son is born. The love that can be felt for a child born to you, the love your spouse can have for that child, the love between each of you, for each other, on such a momentous moment. The fire in your breasts this can enkindle for both of you. We are just people living their lives whether now, 2,000 years ago, 3,700 years ago. No matter what the culture, (we are) experiencing our human life that God blesses us with, experiencing the flow of life."

The Egyptian experience is becoming more real to me [Ann] today.

Our legacy lives on in love, our love is our legacy.

~Jeshua

Asenath said more: "We loved each other. He is such a proud father, a good father. He took time for his family and cherished them. The demands were many, but our time as a family was our time—enjoyed and appreciated. He had such power, but you wouldn't know it, his empathy, compassion, his gentleness, generosity. You loved then, Ann."

Jeshua said that among his lives on earth, he had two children. Then Asenath was shown a baby and it had no clothes on. She thought to put some clothes on it before it gets cold. Then Asenath thought, It looks like a newborn, not very old. She saw Joseph with his back to her, holding the babe. His shoulders and back were moving some as strong feelings of emotion and happiness ran through him. Their son was born and it meant so much to him. It was an emotional time for him. He felt a strong love for his family.

Again, Asenath speaking: "He had spent such a long time in prison and that he has a family…now…means so much to him. His love for them is very strong. You can't help but feel so much for him also. He lost his family in Israel so many years ago, the ones he had loved, his father. How he wishes his father were here to help him celebrate this beginning. But now he has regained a family again."

With these emotions in play it was a very tender moment for the parents. Asenath could feel the joy in his heart and love in his eyes as he handed the child back to her. She knew he was thanking his God profusely in his heart. Joseph was such a good person, and how lucky she felt to be his spouse.

> *There are many things about love when tenderly nurtured are beautiful.*
>
> *~J*

The days in their life were typical, in some respects even in comparison to today. Soon there were two little ones, preschool age. They were lively. The courtyard was lit with bright sunlight and Asenath and the two towheads were there amusing themselves. Joseph would stop by for lunch and they were waiting for him. Soon he came from the doorway to the left. The two towheads spotted him and the little ones thought, *Another playmate, more fun!* Soon there was tickling and giggling going on. Joseph was a good father, not at all distant from his children. He appreciated what he had each present moment. Rumbling stomachs soon reminded them that there was lunch to be eaten. He picked one child up in his arms and he and Asenath each took a hand of the other child. I watched as together they left to have their meal.

The following scene came to me when Jacob, his sons and their family came to Egypt because of the drought and were finishing their long journey to Egypt. This was in muted shades of the desert and dusty sand colors. Most of the Jacob's family members were on foot. The family was spread out on the horizon. The arrangement was more wider than in depth. They were a tired assortment of folks from their dusty desert travel. There were donkeys with double baskets with possessions sticking out of the baskets. The garments the people wore were flowing robes. A tent with no sides, but with a back, was put up to shade Jacob. Jacob was semi- reclined in the tent with his sons.

Asenath was in an Egyptian carriage behind Joseph. She could see he was about one block ahead. He drove a chariot with a team of horses to greet his family. She saw him embrace his father and brothers in turn. It was a joyous reunion. Then Joseph's wife was to be introduced to Jacob. I saw her get out of the carriage or what was used for transportation. From the side I saw the dark hair with bangs and a headband with some ornament in front. The off-white gown was sleeveless, long, slender, with pleats in the front. There was a bracelet for jewelry and an ornamented belt. She went over, embraced Jacob and each brother in turn with a hug of welcome. Joseph was beside himself with smiles. He was so, so, happy. His Israeli and Egyptian families were meeting and now united.

The years went by and the boys grew into teenagers. Asenath was trying to do a juggling act. She was fulfilling her duties as the daughter of an Egyptian priest as best she could. On the other hand, she was helping Joseph's people the best she could also. If there were goods that were needed, she tried to provide, or if there were small decisions to be made that would help make their life easier, she tried to do that. She had some power to do that. This latter part was not settling well with the higher Egyptian religious priests. Her father had passed away, so he was no longer around to buffer their disturbing thoughts about her. They did not seem to understand that she could respect and work with both religions.

This sounded like today, and humankind has yet to completely learn this fact. Humankind creates war or atrocities over the same God who loves all of them equally.

Even though Joseph had many responsibilities, he took time to get away and relax. Many times, he and Asenath sat together on their porch/patio relaxing and listening to the quiet evening sounds of people and nature. Sometimes when they were quiet, she looked at him and he had turned off the burdens of everyday chatter in his mind and was communicating with his God. He had learned to do this, and it had become more deeply ingrained while he was in prison. This had helped him very much then, as it was helping him now. She couldn't help but feel not only love but admiration and respect for her husband and his spirituality. He taught her much on that subject by word and example.

Joseph had a high position but he knew that even with that, there was no absolute guarantee of safety. Perhaps this is why this later scene was so strong for the couple because of the careful atmosphere that seemed to prevail concerning Asenath's work.

It was daybreak, the start of another day. They were feeling a strong love for each other and exchanged these comments. He said that, even though he won't be able to hold her in his arms during the day, he'd hold her in his heart. She promised the same in return. The Jews and Egyptians believed in life after death. He said that whatever life he lived, his heart will follow her in her lives. She reaffirmed the same commitment to him.

An official arrived and asked him to come. Joseph waved him off for a few moments. He was getting dressed, adjusting his Egyptian headscarf. He touched the center of her chest with his hand and she placed her hand on his chest. They both say "love" together. They were both feeling deeply of their mutual love and then he was off for his day.

She went to the patio outside their bedroom. What would be a railing was a half wall with no roof. From here she could see him walking with a group of men. He glanced back, knowing she would be watching. She stayed there long after he disappeared and longer, just feeling love. Her assistant came and was waved off for a short while. She sat down on the floor, focusing on love, just feeling it. In a short while the assistant came back and softly questioned "love?" to which Asenath said, "Yes." Then she got up and began her day.

Her and Joseph's marriage was close. One of the last scenes of that lifetime that came to me was this verbal exchange.

At the beginning of this third life, I wrote about a shaft of light and the sound of dragging stone. Even with the care she and Joseph exercised for safety, Asenath was tricked into going into a pyramid. I believe she went because they told her Joseph had asked for her and needed her help. That was not the case and she met her fate and passed on in her thirties. She knew some of the Egyptian herbs, plus poisons, and used those to hasten rather than prolong her death in the sealed pyramid.

When all the above was done, I sat down and read the Bible about Jacob and Joseph. I hadn't looked at this story since I read the children's version in fourth grade. I learned more.

I don't need movies to keep me entertained at this point, this is all just too fascinating for me. You can take this for what you want. I'm just recording something for me that is incredible. Inside

I feel comfortable with this. The wondering, the whys, the how comes are settled.

When you think about the above promises, didn't Joseph/Jeshua come through in all those above past lives? Didn't that love follow in all of them? Love is definitely what we take with us from this earth and perhaps is the main ingredient we return with to live a new life on earth. It comes out in different ways as cultures have developed and history is played out.

When I think back over these stories, I always feel better when I find other information to reconfirm them. Julia Ingram is a psychotherapist who has much experience in past life regression. She wrote an article entitled "How Past lives Impact the Present." Here are bits and pieces of thoughts from that article that reconfirm the truth of past lives for me.

- Strong emotions from previous lifetimes sometimes carry over into this life. Because these emotions are tied to events from another life, the emotions don't necessarily make sense to the person experiencing them.
- Powerful emotions (love and hate) can spill over from one lifetime to another.
- Pledges made during other lifetimes now seem like contracts that must be kept.
- Powerful feelings of familiarity and love, strong impulses…
- Strong immediate feelings (affection, love, animosity) toward a stranger indicate a possible past life origin (or a present-life repressed memory).

Jeshua always kept his promise. I told him if he wanted me to be on these excursions, there better be nothing scary, or I'd back out. There has been nothing scary, just a big Wow from me and now gratitude. The following quote would be appropriate here.

> *Please don't doubt so much what I tell or reveal to you. All this is possible. Much of your past lifetime was accomplished as told even though you have a hard time believing it. Believe it; it is true. Now you know why I have chosen you. We have shared and continue to share. Let God's blessings fill your soul beloved.*
>
> *God be with you and I'll be with you.*
>
> *~Jeshua*

"Oh my gosh" is all that I can think and feel as this becomes clearer and clearer to me. Sometimes the love is just there. What I do is enjoy it a while and then think, there must be other people in the world that need love and, by making an intention, I give it away. And you know what? What I gave away is just replaced. That's how God is, a never-ending supply of love.

Confirmation of Joseph's time

I went to spiritual conference in California in the fall of 2000. There were people there with differing abilities, but probably none with a story similar to mine I'm sure but I didn't really want to expose myself or my story that much. This was still confusing for me at that time.

That first night I explained to my roommate my dilemma of wanting a third person to confirm this Joseph story. She was surprised at my story but she was also a very objective person. So she voiced a very well-stated intention of needing a third-person confirmation.

I went to sleep and the intention worked! Joseph came to me in a dream and said he was my third person. We talked of many things, but I focused on my mental debate of being Asenath and wanting to solve this long-standing debate. So he started stating over and over and over again you know this is true, you know this is true, you know this is true. Soon I was saying it over and over with him, you know this is true, you know this is true, you know this is true until I came to the point of knowing and believing I had been Asenath.

I remember this all with deep affection. Again I thought, Someone had to be these people. You read about how many reincarnations a person can have; I just didn't know it was going to be me in these instances.

The angel in the book *Interview With An Angel* by Steven Thayer and Linda Nathanson stated on past lives they are only brought up if it is needed to help with this present life's purpose. I have translated my purpose or part of it, to share this so it can help or inspire others in meeting their spiritual abilities, consciousness, and loves.

In Glenda Green's book *Love Without End,* adamantine particles are explained. These particles are the smallest particles in the universe and they have memory in them. The adamantine particles are commanded by love only by love. These were the particles of love and memory working in me. In my meditations and sleep I had emotions and events with Jeshua that I couldn't explain, and that he initiated. I was uncomfortable with them and the reasons I would use to explain this away didn't last for very long. The explanation really came from 3700 BC from Joseph. This explained additional factors of my awakening and how I feel about it now.

Today I feel sad for Asenath. She was trying to help the people, no matter their religion, but others couldn't accept that, and she met her fate. Miriam knew that Jeshua's teachings were right and tried to defend him, but the closed minds of those at that time would not open. She met her fate. Rita had a different life; she could practice what she believed because it was accepted. She was able to express her beliefs. It turned out very well for her and for those around her.

In life, all are at varying levels of spirituality and all must be respected at the level they are at. We are all developing in our own way and timing. At this time, the millennium, we have a lot of extra help to do this. The more we express our freedoms and equality to all peoples with love, respect, and truth, the more we pave our road to spiritual evolvement, enhancing humanity and embracing of peace.

In 2015 a friend told me of a new book titled *The Lost Gospel* by two scholarly authors Simcha Jacobovici and Barrie Wilson. This gospel was not choosen to be put in the bible, yet it survived through the thousands of years. There are eighty pages devoted to Joseph and Asenath with copious footnotes. This ancient manuscript goes back to 570 CE and is translated from Syriac to English. The authors used high technology at the British Library to determine the smugged and deteriorated words.

It amazes me how these old scripts survive to be read again but I have a philosophy that there must be some element of truth for it to survive. For me it was interesting to read. I don't recall the incidents except for three. One - Rita and Asenath having bee stories, two - the exchange of hands on Joseph and Asenath chests as a sign of love and respect, three - Asenath not having an interest in Joseph until she met him in person.

Rita's garden continued.

Rita's garden now consists of flowers, steps, fountain, and a gazebo. Sometimes in my visits with Jeshua at the garden, when there wasn't a concern about any big revelation or spoken word, we just enjoyed each other's company. Nearby and in view from the garden, is water. It could be a lake or river, just beyond the steps.

A couple of times we have been there sitting on a marble bench enjoying the view. These words would fit in there:

Do not be afraid to come to me for other than just love. no need for questions and petitions, etc. There needs to be no other requests other than just love. If only others could find their way to this point also. We have been this way through many of your lifetimes. That is why it is so strong. There is no reason to be separate or deny it that is not heaven's or God's way. Do not deny yourself.

~Jeshua

There is a further use of Rita's garden. With the attack in New York on September 11, 2001, I joined with all in prayer on that day and in the days following. Jeshua asked for my help.

I thought, What can I do? Prayer is good, I suggested. He stood there with a questioning look in his eyes.

I said, "Sure I'll help," just trusting him on his request. We were back in the garden and it was filled with souls.

The souls were roundish and I could see through them and, as I looked through them, the colors of the background were much more intense. They didn't appear to be in any discomfort at all, just restful, and relaxing.

Really, heaven is joy and I'm glad that they are enjoying the garden.

I said, "Welcome, stay as long as you want, and trust that God will take care of everything." I didn't know what else to say and was so glad that there was a higher self, St Rita, and angels, and other heavenly spirits, who were handling this part. Remember in the third meditation, Jeshua told her that she helped people with their crosses and incoming souls. This was part of it.

In other cases when a large influx of incoming souls, the garden and many other places in heaven are used and can be changed in appearance to ease their apprehension. It will have the same scenery as they were used to on earth.

The house in the garden

In a few weeks, I was back at the garden with Jeshua again. There were still souls there, but many had moved on to other happy areas. We decided to go to a small house on the knoll. Remember when Jesus asked me what color I wanted my house? It was decided that the color would be of the sunset—blue, white, silver and gold. This was it! This was the house and, here was how the colors fit in.

I could see us go up the walk from the steps to the house. We were in round soul/spirit form not physical bodies. The house reminded me perhaps of a small fifteenth century French house. It was two-story, with a chimney on one end, a blue painted stone exterior, with white cornices. There were three larger double-hung windows upstairs and three downstairs on the side facing the garden. Inside, we looked out toward the garden from a window. I noted how glad I felt that others were enjoying the garden also.

In this room was a large white porcelain fireplace with gold gilt edging over the raised decoration. Now we were in a physical spirit form; Jeshua pulled up an armed chair and sat down. The chair must have been fifteenth century, as it was very straight backed and, in my opinion, could have used a lot more comfortable padding. It was upholstered in a white material with a touch of silver thread woven through it. (Over the past few months I had made friends with St. Germain and Archangel Michael.) St. Germain pulled up a similar chair and Michael sat on the couch. We chatted for a while. I moved to another part of the room as they continued to talk shop. When it was time to depart, Jeshua dematerialized,

Michael went through the wall, and St. Germain stayed as we had something to discuss.

I could never figure out where the door was, but if you can dematerialize or go through a wall, who needs a door?

The final debate

After all the thoughts, emotions, books, a conference, and the feelings I've gone through, do you think I'm done with debating? No! Seventeen months after this all started, I still wanted confirmation of some sort. The ego was still strong for me.

A couple of times I heard, *What do you want?* And I'd reply that I wanted the truth and so they'd start with me again. One time I asked Archangel Michael if this was all true. I had asked him a couple of times previously about this. As clear as a bell I heard, "Would I lie?"

Well, I was at that point where I had to admit to those past lives and other instances if I was to write this story. Repetition throughout my journals that they want this book written was a sign that I was talking with the heavenliest.

Edgar Cayce wrote about the Akashic records. The Akashic records consist of every thought, word, and feeling, event, and deed of each person in every lifetime. These records are kept on the heavenly side of all the lifetimes we have been through. Cayce was able to access these records when he did his readings. Today there are people who are also able to do so. In my mind was the thought of getting additional confirmation on these past lives through hypnotherapy and through the Akashic records.

I found someone I thought would be reputable to look into the Akashic records for me to double check on these past life stories. I wanted to be accurate and didn't want to write anything that was wrong or from ego. As this channel started to reach for the Akashic records on my behalf, she met a being with firmly folded arms that said this would not be allowed.

She told me this was unusual; it had only happened a couple of times to her. So I tried this question, *How can I best accept these lifetimes?* To me Jeshua is too large a figure for me to think I actually had these parts to play in his life.

Now the voice from beyond became forceful and said, "Every time you don't believe this is like you are slapping Jeshua in the face. Every time you deny this, is like you are slapping him in the face. Every time you refuse to believe this, is like slapping him in the face."

I felt like I had been slapped in the face three times, because I would never, never want to do that to him. The woman said that the voice wasn't speaking angrily, as they don't get angry in heaven, but were just being forceful in trying to get the point across. She said this was very unusual for her that they would speak in this manner. There's that word again: unusual.

Hmmm, this is an unusual story. Again, I am told to write down my conversations with Jeshua, to write of extraordinary things happening to ordinary people. I rest my case, here it is. There will be more and more breakthroughs of people being able to relate to the heavenly world by hearing, sight, feeling, and knowing. This is one of them.

After the above forcefulness happened, I felt pretty timid about talking to the heavenly side, after all this is the divine. Any boldness I had evaporated and I felt like tiptoeing around Jeshua. I still wanted to converse with him, but felt very timid about doing it. Well he knew this and came from the angle of love. I felt comfortable with that and soon things were back to normal. He did mention that we got our point across and I wholeheartedly agreed. He added if I wanted to go into the Akashic records, he would go into them for me.

> From Jeshua: *Come, drink, fill your soul with my insights. Give praise to your creator and pray for others that they will do the same. We are all one and need to pray and love and work together for everyone's benefit. Remember this, that one soul can benefit many others by just their prayers. Can you imagine if all do that? God is very generous and good*

and desires so much to not only share his blessings but to also be acknowledged and loved by mankind.

I asked Jesus for input on prayer and this was his message.

Tell them that my love for them is complete. Love not only makes the world go around but also the universe and heaven. It is the building block, being that it is God. Turn their attention heavenward several times a day. I don't mean an "Oh God" just in surprise or as a reaction. Listen to others that are coming out more and more on the spiritual side. All were in anticipation about the 2000+ millennium. It wasn't that at the stroke of midnight things would happen, but it is a gradual change. Not to be alarmed as change is normal. The best change is that everyone will focus more on the spiritual. Look to your young people they know. You can guide but they'll also point out to you new aspects. That is fine, as they will be higher tuned into heaven.

~Jeshua

Always have faith, trust, and hope, my loved ones. Earth is just passing scenery for you as your real home is heaven. We hear and are guiding you. Please understand how much we want to be of help while you are on your earth visit. After all, you did ask for our help before you came. Ask now to receive.

~Jeshua

We love you and do come if you ask. We accept your free will. God will always provide; have confidence in that. There are many good items in your religions, to help you bring your heaven on earth. Let them be your beginning teachers and we will direct you.

All love, Jeshua A prayer:

My God, you resonate throughout our world with your love in each caring creation and moment. Move us; help us resonate in your creation for the appropriate use of the gifts you have given us. Help us be aware of your love of us that we may forgive and love ourselves and all others. Love, Jeshua, your son.

We are helping you even though you don't know it. We are with you, have confidence. It'll all be okay. We have happy things planned for you. My arms are here for you to come to... Welcome.

And so that's my story. Incredible to you? Yes. Incredible to me? Yes, but it happened. So in reflecting on my earthly journey, it's been a wonder.

What are you wonders?

Life can be a spiritual journey of the heart.-Jeshua Welcome to my abode my sanctuary of love. Dwell always here, drink, refresh yourself. It is endless as God is endless, my dear. Welcome to your side of heaven on earth.

~Jeshua

Extend your love out to the world, so that when you need it, it will come back to you. Tell the world I love each with boundless love. To come to me that I may blanket them in it. Tell them to have no fear and find only love and be quiet of mind to find me in their listening.

Love always, Jeshua

Interlude

It has now been few years since this started for me. I have had time to reflect and gain new insights from this wonder and amazement, and to integrate it. As many people that read this book, there will probably be that many different reactions. I believe some will love it, some will be confused, and others will call it a fantasy. Would you call this a textbook case of awakening? In a way I guess you would.

I had some fundamentals of religious principles to draw on, yet there was more to learn and there had to be changes in my thinking and heart. Some of what I knew was very right and very true, but there were other principles that weren't quite right. It didn't match with what I was experiencing. I had to look for new answers, different answers, to what was going on.

Jeshua gave me a drop of his energy along with my higher self to make this come about. It's been pointed out we have our own internal guidance system from God. This I have learned to listen to. We need to develop and listen to that more now, and take what we gain from this internal system of ours and balance it out with the outside stimulus of our world.

Sometimes now I sit in church and really listen to what is being said, sung, or presented. I balance that against what I have learned that is new. There will be times when I say to myself, This is very good, this is right on. Then I say to myself, That word could be changed, that sentence could be left out, or that paragraph needs to be dropped.

What I am saying is keep what is good in our religions, and change what needs to change. We as a human race have evolved in our thinking since 2,000 years ago when Jeshua walked the earth, and now there needs to be new growth and change in some beliefs. If we are going to have the thousand years of peace promised to us on earth, we need to look at quite a few things.

In Neale Donald Walsch's book, The New Revelations: A *Conversation with God,* is the direction to look at what does work and what doesn't work. It's about change. We change from birth to death. Nature changes from spring to winter. Change is an accepted fact, and part of our human evolution. Change is also part of our spiritual evolution. We are not the same type of people now than when Jeshua walked the earth two thousand years ago. If he walked the earth now, he would approach some of his teachings to us in a new manner. We actually have this new manner available to us now. We need to come to it with an open mind. I read a quote once that said, the most expensive thing there is a closed mind. Then again, let's add, we need to think not from the mind and ego but from the heart. Do you think the word "apocalypse" means terror and suffering from a God of love? Over the years, words and translations have changed the meaning of the text. It really started out in Greek, then to Latin, to middle English, to what we understand now. In Greek the word "apocalypse" means reversal; to uncover. *We need to reverse our thinking on some things and be open to the new that will be uncovered.* That's what apocalypse really means.

This is the glorious thing now happening to our world, to each individual if we allow ourselves to be open to it from the angels, spirit, and ultimately from God. The change comes from a God of love and joy in our hearts, who wants to give us an unmeasured amount of it, and release us from our self-imposed fears. Our fears make us prisoners, and limit our freedom. Each of us needs to look inside ourselves and replace that fear with the freedom of love and joy from God.

Again, from Walsch's book

1. Functional: what works and what doesn't work? Look at your individual world and beliefs.
2. Adaptable: what are you to change in your beliefs so the world can again function as the peaceful world God provides but humans have messed up?
3. Sustain: when you have made the correct changes from the heart, they'll be sustained because that's where you are meant to be.

Jeshua did this. He said some revolutionary things during his days on earth. He is back with us today with each of us, through our hearts, which is where love is.

Religions? Well, some of us like to eat our meals from paper plates, some from pottery, some from fine china. God likes diversity in all things and that includes spiritual practices. So what difference does it make if mankind gets its spiritual nourishment from different types of plates? It is all given from the same source, and we give it back in the best manner that our cultures leads us to in the acknowledgment of our source, God. He gives to us with love and we give back to him by loving ourselves, our neighbors, and his creation. This involves each individual working on letting their hearts be the master, and the mind be the servant. It takes evolving. It'll be accomplished much sooner if done in unity, love, life, respect, honesty, justice, and kindness to our neighbors and ourselves. If you are doing the correct, right thing, and not from ego or power, this change can be accomplished. Don't worry about the other guy who doesn't understand yet. Just bless his heart, say a prayer, and ask his angels to guide him. Some forget or don't know they have angels to guide them or to call upon. They need our blessings then for their remembrance of who they are. Each is a child of the God, who sent his angels to help us when asked.

Lately, I haven't had the blockbuster experiences like I did at the beginning of this. I have somewhat figured out what is going on. Now that I am not so astonished at visits with Jeshua, it has been a calmer experience for me. It is normal now. Like he said, he is always with us. With this new way of thinking, all these experiences are a joy now, and that's the way life on earth is supposed to be.

Part Two

Tidbits for all of us

We are born with our spirituality intact. With the passage of time, that connection decreases as other world pressures and distractions take place. Religions can give a renewed hint of introduction to spirituality, but spirituality continues on beyond the structure of religion by our own efforts carried on in our hearts. By one's own intentions, a person can gain and stay there in communion with God, Jeshua, heaven, and all. And it is all because of the open portal of love. Without redrawing the wheel, this renewal can be done independently if we take the time to listen to our heart. We need to welcome the spiritual side of us.

I have felt that what Jeshua has said to me, he could also say to you. Many have said that we are all one. In following this belief, I felt the following passages could also be meant for you. These are given in that openness of sharing. What is in parentheses I put there to help the wording flow easier or be more understandable.

The below consists of quotes or experiences on love, spiritual growth, God, children, meditations and visions, life's problems, and miscellaneous tidbits. Some of it may be repetitive. I included repetitions because the heavenly realm will repeat words or phrases until we get the message, besides I have always liked meaningful, inspirational quotes or phrases. Maybe you'll find something that you would particularly like to remember also. Notice that these messages are always welcoming, always loving, always supporting, and guiding. It's a sign of the heavenly, and it is also important to remember that the angels and heavenliest like thank yous and thoughts of gratitude from us also.

Love

The following quote I share first because I want you to feel the depth of Jeshua's love for us. At least that is how it affected me when he said it. I had been very moved by him when he said this.

Jeshua: *I'll wash and baptize you with drops of my love to protect your heart, soul, and body. Remember this for your comfort of soul and happiness and joy.*

And others…

Spirit: *Always, always live from love, as God your creator has given it to you.*

Jeshua: *Go now and share. Our love is their love also, as all are one. Go in peace, start your day.*

Jeshua: *The love within us overflows in harmony and cooperation with the universe, the divine love.*

Jeshua: *God the father directs and never abandons His children. They are His creation, He is part of them. How could He abandon Himself then? Much love abounds in the ethers of the heavens and universe, and much love is directed to the heart to help it open and enjoy our oneness with God, our Father.*

Jeshua: *I love, now love yourself. You are as planned. Where you are is as planned. Your growth is up to you, you are your creator. Love yourself as I love you.*

Jeshua: *With God as the center of your being, always invite Him in, always center on Him. Then being positive is just a natural outgrowth. It's the easiest way in your world. There is your true help. That is my source too.*

Spirit: *Love is uplifting to the ethers of heaven. Breathe its perfume, love it's sight and know your God is love, the love that fills all, that comes to all, that is not ever diminished but only increases. There is no end to it, only expanding abundance. Why (do this)? You are love. The source is within you.*

God: *Be love to all you meet, in the best manner possible. We will direct. Take me into your heart and turn most often to me. I will guide as will my Son and angels (do). My love is ever planted in your heart.*

God: *(on my birthday) Your age is not important to me. What you have done, the thoughts, the love that you hold, matters. Your quote for today says not to rest on things of the world. How true rest with me, let your mind and thoughts travel to me, your home love, God.*

Angels: *Love makes the world go around, the universe unites and heaven responds more than ever. Increase and keep love in your heart. Heart is your source of love since God is there all's source of love and all (there is). Praise God in your quietude; feel, enjoy, appreciate. He will take care of you. Share as your brother Jesus shared. We love you deeply, much love your angels.*

There are many other references of love throughout the book. At times, to come from love, there has to be forgiveness preceding it. A Confucius quote goes something like this, "if you are hating someone or something, dig two graves." One is for what or who you hate and the other for yourself. I talked of each person being of love. Every time we hate or act or say not from love, we are tarnishing or diminishing ourselves. We need to consider the bigger picture of what experiences, we or they have agreed to learn in the earth school. From that point, I like the concept that Course of Miracles puts forth, we always have a choice, even if it's just in our attitude or intention of how we want to receive things

An excellent guide to carry us through difficulty and life was given to us by Archangel Michael. This is for all people of faith or nonfaith. It is found at www.beatpeace.net. The title is Blessings, Giving and Deeds. This free short book says much. It is from the angels point of view of life for us earthly students. Read it a few times, it is not difficult. There are other good titles by this author also listed on this site.

Spiritual Growth Quotes

Jeshua: *(on self-esteem) I accept you the way you are. You don't need to have a higher IQ, be a prominent social wiz, business tycoon, or other worldly evaluations. My love does not judge and neither should yours of yourself. You know yourself what is important the heart, the soul. The mind helps to direct the heart and soul at first but then the heart and soul directs the mind because they follow God's directives. I help all in communion with God. Know this and live. It doesn't have to be a great life on the exterior, just the loving life on the interior that overflows to the exterior. Know, my dear, that you are loved and accepted just the way you are.*

Jeshua: *At this moment, everything about you is whole and complete. Our love (heavens') here does not judge, it just loves.*

When trying to connect with the angels, and to know for sure you are doing this, they give these guidelines.

Angels: *The guidance from us is peaceful and serene. False guidance causes worry and anxiety. True guidance takes a moment to look in and connect. False sometimes just leaps at you it can be ego and illusions. Keep reaching for the true. Do meditations and chakra clearings to bring our guidance through easier. (Don't feel you have to do this alone, always ask the angels for help.)*

When it's from us, you'll know it. It'll feel positive, upbeat. It'll bring joy, knowing you are in the right guidance.

We don't look on the downside. When you feel put down or on the downside, you'll know it's not us.

Angels: *We bless; false (guidance) condemns, or leads to guilt. Listen not only for our voice but pay attention to how you feel. If you feel bad or feel it is not from us, call us in to clear and lift (it away). We will be there always there. Ask for God's golden white light, breathe it in, feel positive, now speak or think. Our guidance is with you then. Our blessings always and guidance on your journey. We love you and love being on this trip with you. Your heavenly friends.*

Spirit *(or angels, Jeshua, God): Love, all love is meant for all, to feel, to enjoy, to anticipate. Correct love can bring freedom of the soul and spirit. It nourishes the soul and spirit to be the best it can be while on this earthly journey. It blesses and nourishes. Open the heart and soul to receive it, pour forth gratitude and thanks. Then spread it around to all you meet, and through prayer, spread it around to those you don't meet. Ask the Lord God into your soul, reflect with him and see him in all things. This is where your God is, in all things thus treat all things with respect and love, and embrace and honor their presence. Give them honor and respect for what they do to enlarge and sustain your life.*

Spirit: *Trust, know, unity, love, honor, respect, honesty, kindness, use thanksgiving. Develop all the above and use at all times with all things you will create the harmony that you desire. You can be one of the lesser ones (by human standards) doing this and you will shine forth in God's gloriousness.*

Jeshua: *You are perplexed where all this is leading? Have confidence that love and joy in my heart for you will keep you centered on where you will be at all times. It is not a time of fear but a time for understanding.*

On reading spiritual books:

Jeshua: *Yes, there are getting to be more out now (published) and they all complement each other. It helps those, such as you, to understand more of your world and my world here, so each can live in further harmony with the other. Their physical selves here, their soul there, but all are one, and one with the universe. Keep reading. Let it draw you more to love me, draw you closer to God, to all that is.*

There has been a prophecy of 1,000 years of peace with the beginning of the new millennium. How is this going to happen when you stop and look at the world? This is how...

Spirit: *Even though we are in the densities of earth (earth has a slower vibration than those of the spiritual realm), our hearts are now being drawn back to their spiritual home of love, of God. This is how we are going to find our peace, each individual, one by one being drawn and raising or discovering their spiritual awareness, their spiritual consciousness. Congratulations and a big welcome to the world of joy you are beginning to now walk. Of the peace within yourself you will now discover. It will give yourself a piece of heaven on earth for you. And as you do this you will find areas of your interior self and thinking transformed. This transformation will then start to be manifest in your exterior actions.*

On Prayer

Jeshua: *The prayers raised to me are like perfumed incense. They open their hearts to me that I may come and dwell in them and bless their souls.*

Angels: *Prayer can be multifaceted and colorful. It can be one way but is best with two-way responses; it's like a conversation then. Not all can see or hear our response but be aware because our response is there. It might manifest right away or you'll have to wait, but always it is answered. Didn't Jeshua say, ask and it will be given? Your intention and thoughts hold so much of the answer. We answer for what is the best good for the person praying. The bad, that is a person's thought forms, and can also manifest. That is their thought forms not ours. The angels.*

We are to help and guide. Always, dear loved one, think positive loving thoughts that are honest, kind, respectful, and forgiving of others and things. We, as all heaven, can see to the bottom of your thoughts, as all is known in heaven. Those in tough situations are there to learn and to grow. They might not think on this earthly journey that it is so, but so it is. Doesn't one come out with new perspective and/or strength through a difficult trial? As hard as it is to believe, before you came on this earth you elected for this. We, on the heavenly side, were asked and do help you here through this. Believe us, dear ones, you are spiritual beings in an earth costume suit that came down for experiences that only this planet can give. You were willing and had no fear from the perspective of heaven because you know you will return there that much more experienced, wiser, and evolved.

Angels: *Prayer, turning inward and meditating, will be your guide as you seek our consul. If the consul you receive is loving and repetitive, you can be sure it is us. Then look and be aware around you. Do not only look for opportunities to help but to be helped. Sometimes you are serving a purpose for another by being helped, but also be responsible for yourself* in the best manner possible. In all areas of your life, stand for your truth. Love always your angels.

Jeshua: *Yes, the Holy Spirit is good for you now. You are becoming more acquainted with him. He always guides and directs in according to who you are. My little one, depend on him often as I did. You consider God your source, the Holy Spirit is part of that source.*

Miscellaneous Topics

Jeshua: *You consider my presence and communication joyful and happiness. I consider my communicating with you joyful and happiness. Love is in it all like an ember, ever glowing and drawing all to its warmth.*

Jeshua: *That's what heaven is enjoy in joy.*

Jeshua: *My glory is my Father. Your glory is also your Father. Now in your awareness you see we both have it from the same source. From the Father who is love the glory is love, is felt as bliss. Tell those you meet, do by your word, action, and intention of this glory that is also theirs. That the unbelieving will believe, not just to think it, but to feel and to listen. We are with all, not to despair. It is only a veil that is on earth. That can be parted by their ever-increasing awareness of God's love for them, to share with them always as they are of Him. No forgiveness is necessary on His part as He sees all without fault. He knows and His knowing is all kindness, gentleness and mercy. He sees in no other way. Praise to you and praise to our Father. Thank you and spread the good news. Love always*

Jeshua: *Let us talk about India. It is no coincidence (there are no coincidences) of you picking up the book on India and reading it. It is to expand your awareness, to appreciate, to know that all sincere world religions approach the same God in their own manner (There are many paths to God). But let it not be thought that only their way is correct. All ways to God can be correct. All ways must be acknowledged with respect, courtesy, and understanding. They may seem strange to you, but is not... your culture also strange to them? Just a knowing of it is fine; you do not need to understand all.*

Wouldn't the God of all creation put similarities in these religions? It comes from one source and gives back to the (same) source. Praise God all our source and more.

Jeshua: *Forgiveness wipes the slate clean of impurities, (so) that only goodness can prevail. Whenever in a tight spot, do forgiveness. Forgiveness that I and it (forgiveness) may prevail and alter that spot.*

Jeshua: *Love is the basis for us. It is the basis for them (all humans), but they do not remember. Forgive them in their non-remembrance. Yes, we all are safe in God. That has never changed. You are in illusions (the world). Pray through them, feel them with peaceful prayers. Your intentions and feelings hand over to the angels and to me.*

Angels (on death): *Life is a seamless transition from the physical– realm–to the spiritual. Therefore you have no sense of urgency.-Jeshua said the transition at death from physical to spirit is easy.*

Purgatory

Jeshua wanted me to write this. I agreed with hesitation. This is what I experienced. "Okay I'll write it but…to say you (Jeshua) took me there so I could feel and see it. I wonder myself, but here it goes."

It's not for everyone—just those who do not believe in God. It is not to be feared and the stay is not very long. It depends on the individual, what they expect and what they accept. Most stays are just a few earthly seconds. What I experienced was a pure white room, all you see is white. You definitely feel alone. What I felt was the worst for me because there were not even the angels or Jesus to converse with, and they have now come to be a close part of my everyday life through whatever dimension I happen to be in. However you are being closely monitored even though you don't know it. Any recognition and acceptance of God is heralded. It opens the door for the soul to then know God and with love. And then it's over, that's the end of purgatory for that soul. I know I didn't like it. Not to have any feedback from my heavenly friends up there. It is up to each individual to find and acknowledge the higher source of God within himself.

In hindsight regarding the above: I feel when you go to someone's house, you acknowledge the person whose house it is. This is no different. You go to heaven you should acknowledge it as God's and everyone's heavenly home.

> Jeshua: *Have no fear of me being mad at you when it (ego)swells up. I know you don't mean it. It is those who mean it that have my concern. Your thoughts can control so much. If they only knew and took to heart that this is the basis for their actions and in the long run can be the start of prayers and betterment of their spiritual life. Thoughts lead to prayer and prayer can become the nourishment of your spiritual life. There are many different phases of a person's life on earth that*

need nourishment. Prayer is the main one, the basis for all the others. That is an important point.

There are some things about prayer that we are not aware of in our culture. I'll put in just a few quick comments on it.

Number one. A prayer said with feeling and focus is the best. It is heart-centered then and not mind-centered. If pleasant weather is wanted, focus on the warmth of the sun and not cold rain. Feel and enjoy that warmth on your skin.

Number two. Keep in mind how a prayer is said. A request prayer needs to be said in the terms that it is already accomplished. Say, yes thank you (God/angels) for having this accomplished already. It's important to remember how the prayer is said, bring feeling to it, and say thank you - gratitude.

Number three. There is such a thing as mass conscious prayer that has been proven in studies. If a large group of people focus their prayers all at the same time on one subject and at the same time for the highest good of all with grace and ease, then the subject of their prayers will change to the way it is to be. This needs to be done not only with their thoughts but also with visualizing what they want, not what they do not want, as mentioned above. There is one study done on this about crime, and at the time of prayer the crime rate then decreased. Of course I will mention, when it comes to death and that person's soul contract says it is time to go, then they will go. They have accomplished what they are supposed to have accomplished. This is one reason why Mother Mary says *pray, pray, pray*. We need to get this mass consciousness of prayer going in our day for our own and the world's betterment.

I do with you and all creation I know your higher self, heart, and soul—these are on this plane as is your true self. These I react to and sustain in love. On earth you deal with ego (and physical self). It makes it difficult for you, that's why knowledge of this plane is so important. It gives and helps the three dimensional one, it helps you understand the three-dimensional one. I am with you always as I am part of you and you are of me. Always remember to call upon that part of you, your God, your help; love to love my creation and creators (you). Love you, God

In the Course *In Miracles* book, a question was to ask the Holy Spirit what God's will is for you. The answer started from spirit and ended with God.

Spirit: *To share, to love, to be one with God and with all. To honor yourself, therefore, you honor God, to be the best you can be for yourself and others. To accept yourself, work through situations you are in for your glory. To trust always in all ways his will for you. Nothing is lost and recognize all is given. Part the veil between heaven and earth for yourself and help others do the same. Love, love, and love—God*

God: *Love is the source, the source is love. Ann, write this down—energies of the earth are diminishing and increasing all the time. My favor is upon all. Their circumstances are part of their karma that they don't understand yet. Yet, where they are right now, are where they are suppose to be. The best karma of all for any of them is my love for them. Their karma expands and opens up when they can return it (love). Bless each other with love, which is my love also and let the music of heaven sing for them. Each and everyone is needed, wanted, and loved on earth and heaven. Heaven's blessing my dear to you—God*

I, your God, loves you—do not be mistaken about any of that, in any situation you find yourself. All is planned for your glory—yes, on earth too—if you will let it. Your glory is meant to expand from the inward you to the exact present day you are in. Your mind and this illusionary world will defend your thinking but that is external.

Come internal little ones, my invitation. Hear my voice, my angels' voices. My creation, ME, whispers to your soul. Listen—my love for you it is always constant, always there. Let my external creations lead you to your and my internal creation. To your holy moment of our meeting. All love—God

God: *I am on every plane, from the smallest spec of infinity to the largest cosmos of infinity. There you will always find me. This is me in my true grandeur and I love myself from my smallest to my biggest. Now reflect on this. Where you will see me and how, with and in love, I do not end. If you love me as you say you do, use love with all you see, say and do. This is how you'll treat me. Always alight with love.*

My gentle rain, my gentle love falls on all, nourishes all body and soul. I am love, return to Me often. My beloved Son so directs this, he knows it is all's resting place—their true home. You have reached a point and realize this. Not all have. Pray, work with others who are so blinded yet. Now and then they can see my glory and are grateful for it. Help them to increase these times. Their lives will change if each day they look with gratitude at whatever insignificant event and say thanks, direct it to God—me. Then also at injustice they say with a whole honest heart—I forgive. Then with daily practice will they begin their peaceful journey inward. My gratitude and love dear one - God

Sometimes prayer is answered in unexpected ways or events. There is power in our prayers and thoughts from the heart, and we can then be proactive and not passive.

About God and other topics

The following conversation took place when I was thinking about how to approach and converse with God. Jeshua gave me these comments.

Jeshua: Your question?

Ann: Where do I start? Do you want to do what I consider a biggie?

Jeshua: Let's try it, and it is....

Ann: You had me write yesterday of me to center on God, that he is my source.

Jeshua: *That's right.*

Ann: How or what is the best way of doing this?

Jeshua: *You have already done it, my dear. I believe your question has more to do with how much, when, etc.*

Ann: *That to. Please explain.*

Jeshua: *Happy to. You know about centering yourself to go within, correct?*

Ann: Correct.

Jeshua: *That is how you connect with God. I noticed your delight in His answering you yesterday when you did the Course in Miracles exercise.*

Ann: That was so neat! Every time I asked the question, He gave me an answer. I like that.

Jeshua: *Is that so unusual?*

Ann: Well, I have felt he has answered me but just now and then. There he did all the time. I guess there have been times when I'd ask and just felt nothing happened. I'll admit I can still feel intimidated by whom I'm talking to.

Jeshua: *Ann, Now don't go into that, we got you over the hump, stay over it. DEFINITELY.*

Ann: I will, I will.

Jeshua: *Part of why you maybe didn't hear Him is because you felt intimidated. He doesn't want to scare you, just love you. Okay, understand that?*

Ann: Yes

Jeshua: *So ask Him anything, center, and expect and then feel his love grow and expand in you. It'll happen and the answer will come too. You can hear him so much better now. As to how often—as often as you wish. Look at me and I know you feel you inundate me with questions or conversation. I do not grow tired of it and always welcome you. God is even more so over me and endless. He does not grow tired, is completely understanding and patient with your questions and learning. He only approaches from love, not fire or brimstone. He loves his creation, which is an essential part of Him. How could he react except from the Father or Mother mode of love then? Go to Him anytime you wish; I had to and I did. He is my source and if you apply this, He is your source too! Ask Him, don't be timid. You know that I will understand; he is so much more than I. Do so, my dear, that is your source at any and all times.*

After I got over my initial surprise of hearing answers from God, He gave me added boosts of gladness. Here are some.

God: I have sustained you in your efforts, whether you are conscious of them or not. It is an ongoing harmony or dance I do with you and all creation to help; I love to love my creation and

In the fall, the birds gather in groups of hundreds in the trees before they start the annual fall flight south. They make a loud chorus together in their large groups in the treetops, saluting fall and saying goodbye.

God's thoughts on this: *As each little voice of each little bird chirps, so do I behold each voice of each human—held in the highest regard, in highest love by Me.*

A New Outlook

January 1, 2001—New Year's Day. Now that I am more than a year into this new awareness, when I wake up in the morning I usually say a prayer for peace before I even get out of bed. Sometimes I am by myself and sometimes I am joined by angels, or Jeshua, or St. Germaine, or a couple of times by many. St Germaine was Joseph, Jeshua's earthly father. Whoever wants to can lead the prayer. This morning there was only St. Germaine. I thought, *Well, Jeshua must be busy somewhere. St. Germaine wants to lead the prayer and I agreed.* He started out and then Jeshua came on the other side of me so I was between them. Jeshua joined in synchronizing with the same words as St. Germaine. The strength of their voices rolled together over the surface of the earth like thunder. It was terrific. There was such power, strength, love, unity, and earnestness that is in their peace prayer for the world on this New Years Day. It went like this.

"May the peace of God, the love of the universe, be in the universe and within the focus of man. May man learn of his

> *universal consciousness and thus bring peace to himself, to free himself from the dense limitations of earth to the spiritual joys and peace bestowed on him by his Almighty Father. Peace, his Father says to him, come to Me, to your understanding of love, forgiveness, and compassion."*

I was in awe. I felt like a twig between two giant redwoods with this powerful prayer. The one thing about this though— as earnest, sincere, and loving as this prayer was, it can only happen individually, one person at a time each one of us not only repeating their prayer but also acting in that manner. That's our free will. They can't force this on us; we have to find it in ourselves, one by one.

As of now, I find we are on a balancing scale in the world and its events. I see it as though humanity is on the pinnacle of a mountain. On one side is the new awakening, like what I am experiencing. On the other is the old way of thinking. And up ahead near the peak is the spiritual awakening that is going to happen to all, but at different times. In our wavering on this pinnacle of old thinking or to new thinking, each individual will determine for himself or herself how difficult it will be. This can be done consciously or unconsciously. This can be any conflict, big, small, new, or old. What can we do? I believe in proactive prayer to solve a problem before it even starts.

Mother Mary at Medjugorje said, "You have forgotten that through prayer you can stop wars, and you can alter the laws of nature…."

I prefer an easier way of life and change. I choose proactive prayer. It works. It brings results, but on the world scale we are talking about, it'll need so many, many constant prayers on the same subject, at the same time, to bring it about. We can do it, look at the prayers throughout the world that were offered on and after 9/11. Let's not make it so we need a tragedy to bring world unity. Let's do it now before the human race gets into more difficulties than we can handle.

A good example of healing prayers and intentions came to me one morning before I was fully awake. I had these ideas/ thoughts/ insights about prayer, troubled areas, and disasters in the world. Consider the Mideast. There's fighting there, there are leaders and/ or citizens that want peace but there is an element that evidently does not. Above the Mideast I saw something like a black smoke, light not dense, but churning. These were people's intentions, the ones who do not want peace but cause fighting and disharmony. How can help come? In Europe or other parts of the world, there were bright spots of yellow smoke, like areas where people were praying with intentions held for Mideast troubles. Slowly, like an air current this pleasant yellow smoke drifted over to Israel, people's prayers to aid the Mideast in their troubles. You can look at this black smoke, yellow smoke, or clouds as people's intentions joining in universal energy. In this case we just need a whole lot of yellow smoke to dilute the black. The example was on an international scale, but on a smaller scale it can be used to help with family squabbles, personal disagreements, or an election. All these squabbles, fights, disasters, and problems have a different color smoke, or cloud, but the prayer always stays light, loving, and hopeful. We all need hope, we all need prayers, and we all need to just do it.

One time I asked Jeshua to ask God to be merciful on those on earth undergoing their life experiences.

> God's answer: *It is their choice of how hard their lessons will be. My love, compassion, and mercy are always with them; it is in them. The degree of difficulty is determined by how little or how large they open their hearts to me or to the words of my messengers.*

Because our thoughts are powerful, we must always be consciously aware of them. We always have choice of what type of thought/intention to choose. Our thoughts, feelings, and intentions, whether verbal or nonverbal, matter of choice. The saying, "Watch for what you ask for because you may get it" is very true. What our mind is focused on, is what we will get. We do it by default much of the time. Let's say we focus on an event and say or pray "No I don't want this to happen, I don't want this to go that way," and we keep focusing on the negative. This will give us more of what we don't want. Instead, we need to focus with feelings on the positive like this: "Yes, what I wanted is already accomplished, is done. I feel so glad it is accomplished, thank you." This is where our emotions are helpful. The emotion of joy, happiness, relief, and thankfulness are beneficial. Ask for the highest good to come with grace and ease, then we can get the positive results we want. It takes being aware of our thinking in order to change this around, but it can be done. That's why Jeshua says stay with the positive and find things to be thankful for. The answers will come, maybe not right away or in the manner expected, We need to drop expectations and just trust they know how to work it out. And as Jeshua said, where two or more pray together there I am. The more that pray with us the stronger our prayer becomes.

If possible, remember to focus on the bigger picture than just our own small private world. The more often you practice this mindset, the easier it will become.

> God: *All my glory shines forth in my creation, in love, and respect for all. It is my gift to you for your pleasure. When it doesn't seem like pleasure, remember it might be for your growth. Step aside from the problem to look at it. And as you do, ask my angels and this side to give you insight to the problem. Remember to do all from love. In that manner, you will do the best for yourself and for others or the situation. It'll pass. My love dear God. Call on us anytime you need a boost.*

Jeshua: On a problem—Do you trust God? Yes—me. Then put it in his lap. He knows what to do. Trust him as you trust me.

Angels: *With the love in your heart, you are never alone.*

Spirituality *on earth is a step forward to our heavenly home.*

I've learned when we are in bad moods, we are then indeed alone. We shape our thoughts and actions on our own; angels do not participate in negative thoughts or actions. A person then is leading with their mind and not the heart. We need to develop the habit of noticing our thoughts so our heart is the leader.

Jeshua: *Whatever form or person you have been on earth does not matter, as long as it is blanketed with correct spiritual love.*

Jeshua: *On handling confusion or motivation. Get up and exercise more. Not only to lose weight but to get the endorphins going for a positive attitude. Pray don't get disgusted with us. Sometimes understanding us and God's workings are difficult. We know you are trying keep praying, trust, and have faith. Yes, ask for concrete evidence to match what we are saying. Always stay in tune to your thoughts and feelings. Remember we love you through all this. We know your love is returned. Love is the cement (the binding element).*

Jeshua: *Doubt is always seen in man's mind. The reason is his earthly life. He has trouble seeing the secure knowledge of the visions from heaven. He is now going to have to cultivate his sixth sense (intuition). His every increasing bond with heaven will lessen the doubt and along with it will go the confusion.*

Have *I not said we are here on earth to serve one another? Because each one has the spirit of God in us—and in the standpoint of loving God, we then serve one another.*

Depend *on this love that you have, and always seek, serve, ask, request in your doubting and confusion. We will always whisper in your ear our answer, our love, our reply—that will dispel your doubt and give you confidence.*

Jeshua: *Despair can come despite good intentions. Trust and confidence in us is needed, in your higher self. All of this is to guide you through (your life, your experiences). And the idea of handing it over to us is right also.*

Yes, the inner self/intuition is our whispers to you and I know you believe in earnest we wouldn't guide you wrong. Follow your intuition and your success is assured.

Jeshua: *Your confusion is the result of not completely turning it (this problem) over to us, to God. You still have concerns of the future even though we have told you not to. Relax on this my dear.*

Jeshua: *The events of your life have flown as they should. Yes, even the hardships were asked for. Yes, the love, prayers, and guidance, the joy and peace you now have, are freely given. Our Father is in it all through and the Holy Spirit. You are safe.*

Spirit: *What a person is closest to is where they or you draw inspiration from.*

Angels: *Today I begin a new timeframe. Today God and the universe blesses me anew. Today we angels are more than delighted to help you when you call upon us. Today is complete, as all eternity is complete and perfect. As your life mission continues and unfolds, one step at a time in God's love, joy and happiness. Peace.*

Angels: *My dear one, your faith and desire in following your path is gloriously correct and lovingly laid out for you. Have confidence and no doubt pray to us, your guides, Jeshua, Holy Spirit for that. Lovingly, Your Angels*

Angels: *Your glorious understanding and increased awareness of our oneness brings some of heaven down to earth. When all understand this and act it out, their thoughts, feelings, and love, then it will be heaven on earth. Enjoy your day, we are with you, guiding always. Ask us often for it your loving angels.*

Coincidental Miracle

I know that heaven is working with us all the time and if we open ourselves more and ask, they'll be able to do more to help and guide us. There have been times for me where it is uncanny how things work out.

It is said there are no coincidences. The following is one such story that I believe you will find interesting: My friends and I planned a summer trail ride with our horses—an eleven- hour drive pulling the horse trailers. While on the road, one of the trailers lost the electrical connection from their trailer. It had fallen out and got rubbed off on the highway. While looking for repairs and through the road construction, I got separated from the group. I figured I'd catch up to them, but with the road construction I never did find them. There was over half the drive to go yet and I wanted to keep moving to reach our destination before dark. I knew they were going to continue on the interstate but I chose a two-lane, more direct highway because I didn't care to deal with semis and my pulling a trailer at high speed. I'd join up with the Interstate later on and hopefully find our destination ranch by myself. During this time I had no contact with the other trailers; cell phones were not in wide use yet. My daughter was along and was the navigator. After three hours of driving, she was sleeping and I saw a sign to get back on the Interstate so I turned left. This ended up not to be the correct turn but my sleeping navigator wasn't awake to tell me. I knew I would feel more comfortable finding the others, because now it would be dark when I got there. I didn't cherish the thought of getting lost, driving strange roads, or trying to turn around in the dark with a horse trailer. Well I figured I'd turn around at the first gas station. My daughter, who was awake by then, suggested we fill up the gas tank and take a break. Just as we were about to leave the station, in pulled my friends with their trailers! Now talk of angels planning coincidences! What were the chances that we'd be there at that time, in that particular town on the Interstate, at that particular gas station, so that we should all meet again? After all, I had gotten separated, made wrong turns, and there had been no contact between us at all. Heavenly help is so neat. I bet the angels had a chuckle over that one. But now we were all together again, trying to find the ranch in the dark. There are usually stories to tell with horse outings, and this was one of them.

Dealing with inappropriate presences

Someone once asked if I ever had any bad experiences with intuitive work. There was just one time, and it wasn't that bad. This was in the beginning for me, before I knew to ask for protection from the angels and to ask who is speaking.

I felt a presence was near. This presence felt like a military discipline. I felt as though I better suck in my gut (good luck), throw my shoulders back, and do twenty push-ups on demand (good luck with that one, too). I figured this was one I'd just have to bear with.

The following day I was uncomfortable enough to turn around and ask the presence, "Don't you ever come from love?" Love is all I have ever felt from above and, with this question, the presence was gone.

I was trying to think of who the presence could have been. I knew that Archangel Michael was always shown in military garb, so I was thinking of him. But both he and Jesus later told me, "That's not how we work." I believe that, and didn't carry it any further.

I see Archangel Michael as a protector and giver of strength, the same way I see my angels. Do not hesitate to ask your angels for their help in any situation—good or bad. If there is an unwanted presence, ask the angels to carry it to the light. The presence cannot be there if it is not in alignment with your free will.

Children and grandchildren

> Jeshua: *All come to earth to unfold in their journey to God. As much as there is external in the world, it is most important to teach the internal to these little ones. Then the externals of the world will naturally fall into place as it should—full of God who is love. Much peace to you, little ones on your journey.*

All of us want what is best for our children. With our babies and toddlers, they are so close to heaven still that their spirits can still talk with heaven. This is their sixth sense. If we don't shut down their sixth sense, this will be an important tool for giving them the best in this life. As a result they will have guidance, not only from us but also will understand and receive more from their higher self and the angels, for the betterment of their spiritual, emotional, mental, and physical welfare. What a grand start for them to make a wonderful world!

Many times young children claim to have imaginary playmates. This experience is not imaginary to them. When children are born, because they are still so closely connected to heaven, they (to varying degrees) hear and/or see the heavenly side. The influences of this world have not set in yet. As time progresses children are usually told to stop using their "imaginations" in this way. So this fine-tuning they had with heaven diminishes over time by what they see, or are told, or are influenced by.

I had a surprise awakening to this sixth sense that children have in the beginning, when my grandchildren started making their appearances in this world. I did not realize this awakening would give me such an added dividend, but so it did. It also provided me with another motivation to start reading to figure out what was going on.

After my grandson was born, I was in the hospital, holding this ten-hour-old newborn. Looking at his face and tiny hands I heard, "Oh, I'm so happy to be here, I'm so happy."

He was beside himself in happiness, just jumping in gladness to be alive and here. "I'm so happy," (long pause) then a loud exclamation, "Grandma!"

I looked at this little being of flesh and thought, What is this? I remembered that introduction and surprise especially because that was the first time I was connected with the spirit of a new little one.

Several months later, my first granddaughter was born. After what happened with my newborn grandson, I decided to try to contact this newborn. Again I was in the hospital, admiring the few-hours-old infant, and I mentally asked,

What do you have to tell me?

Nothing. I tried to encourage her again two or three times. Finally I heard her sleepy, slow, tiny voice say, "I'm so tired. I've been through so much. I chose my mother and my father because they would be good parents."

Let me assure you (a few years later), she is not slow or sleepy anymore.

Much later on a second grandson was born. I was more relaxed with channeling by then, so here was this newborn's spirit message.

Dear Mother and Father, I love you. I've loved you before I was born. We have had grand memories before, and will again. The grand love of God is in you as it is in me. Thank you for your gift of life that I may now express it and thank you that I may now help you to do so also. Isn't it a joy?

Much love to you, and to my beautiful family.

I find that a beautiful message! (and not just because I'm a prejudiced grandmother).

What I find particularity interesting is that the family or friends we have around us, we also knew before in other lifetimes. This is not saying all family and friends, but there are some. Their relationships to us at that time could have been sister, grandniece, spouse, best friend, etc., and they might have a direct opposite role in this lifetime. They chose to come with us in this lifetime to help us have and experience what we need, or maybe we help them with what they need to experience, or maybe both are true. That is what happens when we reincarnate. We can change our personalities, IQs, culture, looks, gender, abilities whatever so that we will have the experiences we need for our spiritual evolvement.

Further stories are evidence that babies or small children are closely connected to the heavenly side. My first grandson's—mother called it "acting weird" but I interpreted this event thus:

We were sitting together at the family supper table but this three-year-old, with energy, had had enough of the meal, and it was time to run outside to play. In his running, he stopped in the kitchen, bent over by the refrigerator and was looking up at something, we saw nothing there. Then he continued to run, bent over, outside to play.

I thought it was possible that his angel was floating above and going outside with him to play. Thus he was bent over, looking up at his angel and making room for them to go out and play together. (It could happen.)

Early morning is the best time for the other dimensions to contact us because our minds are rested and we are more in tune to their energy. My first granddaughter mentioned above spoke at an early age. When she was two-and-a-half years old, her grandfather died. By now I hope you believe in life after death and loved ones coming to visit you, because he visited her. My daughter previously had made comments about the child having imaginary playmates.

With her grandfather's passing, this young girl came from her bedroom in the morning around Christmastime, saying, "I miss Grandpa."

When questioned why, she replied, "He said he loved me and wished me a Merry Christmas." She took this in a matter-of-fact way, and said it truthfully and innocently from her viewpoint. It was no big deal for her to speak to angels or spirits.

When I was at their house babysitting another time, she ran to the sliding window, looked out and pointed to the sky. "There's an angel, and there's Grandpa," she said.

Later, we were leaving to go to a movie and she was upset that we were leaving without Grandpa. So I told her to invite him along. When we got outside, she ran to the other side of the garage and in a loud voice told him to come to the movie with us. This was real to her. I didn't comment, but just listened.

One other comment on special children that are coming into this world (not just my grandchildren but many other gifted babes): We call them indigo, crystal, or psychic children. They are born with their sixth sense intact, are very intelligent, and are to lead us into the new age. What it took us years to learn, they will already know or learn in half that time. They may act out or not fit in as they try to mold into our three-dimensional world. These children will definitely challenge our educational and governmental structures. The change they will bring about will be for the good of all, not for the separation and duality that is common today. I believe that, if they are going to learn all this worldly information very fast, they will definitely need to know from a very young age about internal character and guidelines as Jeshua mentioned above. This will help them know how to handle social situations and all the information they will absorb so quickly. With them surpassing us in knowledge, the very best we can do for them when they are small is to teach character, morals, values, and spirituality. This isn't to be left just to churches or families, but in all situations that they come in contact with us. We will need to teach those around them peers, siblings, parents, educators, etc., not only how to handle these children, but how to teach and handle themselves around these children. They are very sensitive to wrongs and will be completely frustrated by outmoded systems of education, fake social values, and the dishonesty our current society displays at times. They need to be valued, loved, and understood the best that we can, so that they become valuable contributing members and future leaders of tomorrow's society. The most important groundwork will be to encourage them to continually go internal, to their hearts, to find and use the values that are inherent there. They will challenge us and make us grow also. Look at today's blogs or face book pages, you will see this in big and small ways that it is now being accomplished.

We have to be careful not to drug them, as this would be disruptive to their mental and emotional growth, their brain growth. Otherwise, they'll have to catch up later when they come off the drugs and will not be going through the growth and challenges of changes in their teen years at the same time their peers are. We do them a disservice adding to their difficulties.

They will be able to tell if one is saying the truth, have a sense of integrity toward themselves, and expect no less from others. They will be sensitive to our food additives and pesticides, and prefer to eat vegetables. Other characteristics will be creativity, strong will, and a good sense of humor.

Are all children this way? No, not all. There are more and more books out on these gifted children; pick one up and read it. Professionals working in the area of child development are becoming more and more aware of this shift. Their parents definitely know it. It is one of the millennium shifts coming about. These future leaders are going forward with much compassion to help us. Look at today's blogs or face book pages, you will see this in big and small ways that it is now being accomplished.

> *Jeshua: Children are another of God's blessings on the world. Each one, each soul is moving forward step by step, lifetime by lifetime to its closer reunion with God, learning the many wonderful facets of His love. Each one is blessed with his own special lessons and rewards. The newer children come with many lessons in place to proceed with, but not all of the lessons. The most important and fundamental are of character. Learn those first and the rest will follow more easily.*

Reflections - Rhythms of God's loving care

There are many names we give God. One that he/she likes is I AM. The human body has a chakra system with seven essential chakras in the center; each center has a specific trait. There is much more that can be said about this, and many good books you can purchase to read more.

Here He/She starts with the top of the head chakra, the crown, using His/Her I AM name and goes through the seven main chakras.

> *I AM in the crown that I AM enriching*
> *In the visions seeing*

In the words I AM speaking
Love
In the courage I AM showing
In the body that is working
In the world I AM providing
I AM

The feeling I got after writing that was one of deep security. God is in all, and everything is okay. It just felt good. Now, God, knowing how I was beginning to like these

I AM words, gave me another that is quite simple, but again shows His/Her omnipresence.

I AM in the thoughts of the morning, in the breezes of the afternoon.

I AM in the sweat of the noon sun, in the rest in the evening.

I AM in all.

Analogies

One-time Jeshua came to me with both hands open holding a beautiful white light. This light was symbolic of the light of God that each of us has within us. Gently he blew it into me.

My next thoughts were of a small tent with just one center pole. This pole was God; the roof of the tent was His love. Instead of striped or plain like a circus tent, it was beautiful and symbolic of his love stretched out over all of us, each individual. The colors on his tent were pastel chakra colors, auras of varying intensities. They mixed and moved around so the air seemed colored.

The four outside stakes that stretched out His colored roof were each element we need to live, on the earthly plane. These stakes represented our mental, emotional, physical, and spiritual selves that we need to always keep in balance to get the greatest benefit out of our earthly life.

Each of us has our own tent of God light that is filtered and colorful. I found myself very happy under his canopy, celebrating and thanking God for this love, life, and light within.

Since we are all one, wouldn't it be great to realize that all souls are under this kaleidoscope tent of God's, knowing we are all protected by His love, and understand and give thanks no matter what part of the circus of life we are in? We need the correct mindset so we can all do that.

In India the locust flower is an important symbol. Indians relate this flower to the seventh crown charka, at the top of the head, which opens to divinity and higher consciousness. All I could think of as a comparable flower in my world is the water lily. Of the locust's symbolism, I received this interpretation:

The water lily (man) sits on its big leaf (the earth), and slowly unfolds itself (his soul) as the currents of water (his spiritual life) move. But the opening is beautiful as he steadfastly gazes into the heavens at its creator, with the heart of joy and love.

Everything is pulsating with God's light and love, with his rhythms, whether we humans acknowledge it, ignore it, or I resist it, it happens and even more so in these times.

Finale

The following account is about soul travel. I had not heard of this before, but evidently that term could be used for some of these experiences I've written about. My body stays where it is but my soul goes traveling, and my mind becomes impressed with that travel. These experiences still impress me, but the following one felt like a comfortable working relationship, as though I'd been in that situation before. Writing the words about it flowed so easily for me; I am sure it was the heavenly side's help. Jesus wanted me to write this down. I thought that others might find it foolish, but he said if I found pleasure in it, then others would too. So…

Jeshua and I were standing together high above the southeast corner of the United States. There was not a specific outline of city or river, and no boundaries between nations or states as we might normally think of on a map. From this perspective the earth was very beautiful, whole, and one. Jeshua raised his right arm, opened his hand and maintained that position. From his hand fell medium-size sparkles, like glitter. My higher self-recognized that these were glitters of love, love going to each continent, nation, village, and person's heart. (It enters all, and it would best if each of us acknowledged, focused on, and felt this.)

We moved to an ocean and the glitters of love still fell from his hand. Even in the vast emptiness of the ocean there was love. I raised my arm and opened my hand to see if glitter could fall from it. It did.

You see, there is love in all of us, to give to all. It is to be given, whether it is to human, or animal, or plant, or whatever form of life or nonlife we encounter. God created everything in love and is still part of everything. It is up to all of us to spread the glitter of love around and within our own private worlds, as God and Jeshua give by their examples.

We moved higher above the world, so it was like a globe. The glitter still fell. "The love still falls." (This seemed to be my higher self/soul speaking.) "You see, even as each of us has our own turmoil of life to work through, we are still surrounded by love in this work. And…all is in peace and harmony and love…"

That's the beauty of this scene and of our world. When this is practiced, this is Eden, our heaven on earth. Later, after I came out of this, I wrote, "We are all caught up in our own little worlds. If we can expand that vision and include the spirit world, we would find more love and help than we ever thought possible. The world always has the blessed potential of harmony, beauty, and love, because God put that in all of us to discover and put to use."

Then I heard these words from Jeshua: "As wide as the ocean, as deep as the sea, as blue as the sky, as high as the mountains... for eternity."

Uh, oh, I wondered, *where is this leading?* (My disbelief popped up even then.) But a short time later, I found a children's book entitled *Do you know how much do I love you?* by Donna Tedesco. It had almost the same phrases it in, and at the end of each of the above phrases was, "That's how much I love you." The words that I heard Jeshua say earlier were repeated exactly in this book that we read to our children to show them how much we love them. We could finish each sentence now with Jeshua, God, angels, and the heavenly sphere saying the same thing to you, how much they always loved you, oh child of God.

Another way I looked at these words was to consider the events that I had experienced from the sea there was the dolphin ride; from the sky there was the ride with the horses; from as wide as the ocean is the falling glitters of love. From where I started in 1999 to the mountain I've climbed spiritually to this point, what a climb!

I wish spiritual evolvement for you, too.

In doing the balancing act, here is a clue from the book *Meditations* by Thomas Moore.

Silence is not the absence of sound. That would be to imagine it negatively. Silence is the toning down of inner and outer static, noise that occupies not only the ears but also the attention. Silence allows many sounds to reach awareness that would otherwise go unheard the sounds of birds, water, wind, trees, frogs, insects, and chipmunks as well as conscience, daydreams, intuitions, inhibitions, and wishes. One cultivates silence not by forcing the ears not to hear, but by turning up the volume on the music of the world and the soul.

Consider each lifetime you have had as a jewel: beautiful, shining, and precious. It is strung on a cord of love. This is you and all the other "yous" that have lived throughout time. When we pass from our current lifetime, this strand closes to make a circle with God's love light shining from the center for each lifetime. When we decide to come to earth again, the strand of love is opens again, and we add another precious jewel or the finest pearl of that lifetime.

Every individual has these precious jewels strung on the strand of love. And each jewel or pearl is a closer step to God—these are the stepping stones for the heart. All our steps can be different, but the ultimate goal for all is reaching God. There is no other like you. The contributions you make to earth, no other can make. Remember who you are, a perfect child of God.

I hope you agree with me that I had some good authors with this book. They're the best, and so I'll let them have the last word. My love and joy to you.

> Jeshua: *The love you feel in your heart is universal. It is there for all in the universal awakening that is coming about. Tell all to look about, notice and observe subtle changes occurring in thoughts, in lives. It is not just others' lives but to also look at your own. It is glorious, as I said in the beginning of this book in the beginning wonder and at the end glorious. The glory is available to have on earth now, from each atom of your being to each event of the day. Look for the good in all and everything. Evolve, think, and give thanks to God. There is always something to give thanks for—hold the positive. We come to all in love. Please receive it, absorb it, become a part of it, and then extend it to all. Your loving J.*

> God: *The peace of my love surrounds every heart. It can be felt, my presence, in their heavenly awareness, even when there is no peace in their illusionary world. Tell them to enter there (their heart) and find me.*

> *Like a twittering bird, a shaking leaf, the world is coming alive to itself, which is ME. All my love is poured into each single particle as it makes various wholes. Each is giving glory*

to all around it, recognizing me, the I AM. Ah such times, such moments, and you, my spirits, such creators. Welcome back to my fold of love; you were never lost. This is the great remembering. Ah, the beauty of each soul lighting up, you are my love dividing, multiplying, and pouring forth. The blossoming, the multitudes, the joy, the heaven remembered on earth. Come little one rejoice all is as it should be. Ahhhh, Your God with much and all love.

Bibliography

Blackburn Losey, Meg MscD, PhD. *The Children of Now.* New Page Books, 2007.

Braden, Gregg. *The Isaiah Effect.* New York: Three Rivers Press, 2000.

Foundation for Inner Peace. *Course in Miracles.* New York: Penguin Books USA Inc., 1996.

Furst, Jeffrey, Ed. and Edgar Cayce. *Edgar Cayce's Story of Jesus.* New York: Berkley Books, 1976.

Green, Glenda. *Love without end.* Fort Worth, Texas: Heartwings Publishers, 1999.

Hardin, G. W. with Joe Crane. *On the Wings of Heaven.* Dream Speaker Creations, Inc., 1999.

Hoppe, Geoffrey. *The Shaumbra Symptoms.*www. crimsoncircle. com. Golden, CO, 2001.

Ingram, Julia, and G. W. Hardin. *The Messengers.* New York: Pocket Books, 1996.

Montgomery, Ruth. *The World to Come.* New York: Harmony Books, 1999.

Moore, Thomas. *Meditations.* New York: Harper Collins, 1994.

Roth, Ron. *The Healing Path of Prayer.* New York: Three Rivers Press, 1997.

Thayer, Steven and Linda Sue Nathanson, *Interview with an Angel.* New York: Dell Book, 1997.

Tedesco, Donna. *Do you know how much I love you.* New York: Simon and Schuster Children's Publishing, 1994.

Virtue, Doreen. *Divine Guidance.* Los Angeles: Renaissance Books, 1998.

Walsch, Neale Donald. *The New Revelations: A Conversation with God.* New York: Atria Books, 2002.

Weilbe, Wayne. *Medjugorje, the message* Brewster, Massachusetts: Paraclete Press, 1985.

What the Bleep @@??>!! *do we know, (inspired by the book* What the Bleep Do We Know!?*(TM): Discovering the Endless Possibilities for Altering Your Everyday Reality by William Arntz) DVD, 2004.*

Yogananda, Paramahansa. *Autobiography of a Yogi.* Los Angeles: Self-Realization Fellowship, 1988.

www.ingramcontent.com/pod-product-compliance
Lightning Source LLC
Chambersburg PA
CBHW070318010526
44107CB00004B/353